MONEY MOVES

WAKING YOUR BILLIONAIRE CITIZEN

AARON M. MONTAGUE

MBA, M.Div, MNLP, MTT, MCHt, MSC

Certified Christian Finance Coach

Certified Advanced Christian Deliverance Counselor

Money Moves
Waking Your Billionaire Citizen

A Financial Awakening for the
West Philadelphia Billionaires Society (WPBS)

By Aaron M. Montague, MBA, MDiv, MNLP, MTT, MCHt, MSC
Certified Christian Finance Coach
Certified Advanced Christian Deliverance Counselor

Published by
Kingdom Publishing, LLC
1350 Blair Drive, Ste F
Odenton, MD 21113

Printed in the United States of America.

Unless otherwise noted, all scripture quotations are from the King James Version of the Holy Bible (KJV), public domain.

For information, permissions, or bulk orders, contact:
Montague Motivational Ministries MX3
at MX3motivationalbooks.com

DEDICATION

To my mother, Jeannie Montague, who could take one tired dollar, look it in the eye, stretch it, pray over it, and make it feed a whole house. You taught me how to make "not enough" last until God made a way. You showed me what quiet dignity looks like when the bills are due and the children still eat, laugh, and sleep in peace. This book is my way of saying: I saw you. I saw the juggling, the late nights, the whispered prayers. I saw you make miracles with grocery lists and gas money. May every page of Money Moves become payback, with interest, for every time you went without so that we could have.

And to every mother, father, grandparent, and caregiver who has ever stretched a dollar until it sang—this book is also for you. May the struggle that sat on your shoulders end with you, and the building of generational wealth begin with you.

ACKNOWLEDGMENTS

No book is written alone, and this one is no exception.

To my wife and family—thank you for loving me through every draft, every late-night idea, every "Hold on, I just need to capture this thought." Your patience and faith are part of every sentence in this book.

To the elders who taught me how to stretch a dollar, even when they didn't have the language of "wealth-building"—thank you. You gave me the raw material, the grit, and the fire to say, "We will not stay here."

To the pastors, spiritual parents, mentors, and colleagues who have encouraged the West Philadelphia Billionaires Society vision—thank you for believing that a one-dollar-a-day movement could become a community-owned revolution.

To every client, congregant, and community member who has ever sat across from me and said, "I'm tired of struggling; show me another way"—this book carries your faces and your stories. You were—and are—my why.

To the WPBS founding circle and early adopters—your courage to say yes before everything was polished is the proof that we are ready.

And above all, to my Lord and Savior Jesus Christ—the true Source, the Giver of power to get wealth, the One who turns broken stories into blueprints—thank You for trusting me with this assignment.

"But thou shalt remember the Lord thy God: for it is He that giveth thee power to get wealth, that He may establish His covenant which He sware unto thy fathers, as it is this day."
Deuteronomy 8:18

"A good man leaveth an inheritance to his children's children…"
Proverbs 13:22

FOREWORD

There are moments in history when an idea emerges that refuses to stay quiet.

It begins with a question that challenges the way things have always been done. The vision behind the West Philadelphia Billionaires Society (WPBS) is one of those ideas.

At its heart is a simple but powerful question: *What if ordinary people moved their money with extraordinary intention?* What if students, workers, church members, elders, and neighbors each committed to moving even one dollar a day toward a shared vision of ownership?

What if those dollars did not disappear into random spending, but instead flowed toward businesses, buildings, banks, clinics, schools, and institutions our communities could own and our children could inherit?

History shows that wealth is rarely built by accident. It is built through discipline, organization, and shared vision. Communities that learn to move their resources together change their economic future.

Money Moves was written to help make that shift possible.

This book is more than a guide to managing money. It is a call to financial awakening. Within these pages, Aaron M. Montague speaks not as a distant expert, but as a coach, pastor, and neighbor who understands the reality many people face. Many of us were never taught financial literacy—we were taught financial survival.

We learned how to stretch a paycheck, juggle bills, and simply make it through the month.

But survival is not the end of the story.

This book invites readers to rethink their relationship with money and begin moving from consumer to owner, from confusion to clarity, and from survival to legacy.

For those involved with the West Philadelphia Billionaires Society, this book serves as a practical training manual for building community ownership. For everyone else, it is an invitation to awaken and begin building wherever you are.

As you read these pages, you may hear more than the author's voice. You may hear the echoes of ancestors who built with little and the hopes of descendants who will one day live inside the world your decisions help create.

Real change rarely comes from one dramatic moment. It comes from small, consistent moves made with wisdom and purpose.

So let's begin making those moves today.

— Bishop Antonio M. Palmer
Kingdom Alliance of Churches International

PREFACE

I did not grow up with "financial literacy."

I grew up with financial survival.

I grew up hearing phrases like, "We don't have it," "Money doesn't grow on trees," and "Just be glad the lights are still on." I watched adults I loved juggle bills and stretch every dollar just to make it to the end of the month. Money would come in—and then disappear just as quickly—leaving behind stress, arguments, and that familiar hope:

"Maybe next month will be better."

If that story sounds familiar, this book is for you.

Money Moves was created to help people stop bleeding financially and start building intentionally. It is not just about numbers—it is about changing the way we think about money, the habits we practice, and the future we are capable of creating.

Many of us were never taught how to build wealth. We were taught how to survive. But survival is not the end of the story.

This book invites you to move from drifting to directing, from reacting to financial problems to intentionally building stability, ownership, and legacy.

This is not a book to skim and forget. It is a book to work through. You may want a pen in your hand. You may want conversations around your kitchen table. Some moments may challenge you, and others may encourage you—but if you engage with the process, you will not leave these pages the same.

Preface

For many readers, this book is connected to the vision of the West Philadelphia Billionaires Society (WPBS)—a movement built on the belief that small, consistent financial decisions can create powerful change when people move together with purpose.

But even if you are reading this outside of that community, the principles still apply to you.

Whether you are rebuilding, learning, or simply ready to take control of your financial future, there is a fresh starting point waiting for you inside these pages.

Take a breath.

You are not behind.

You are right on time.

Let's move.

Table of Contents

Wake Up, Builder: This Is Not Just About You

There's a moment that quietly happens in almost every life.

You sit at a table—maybe it's the kitchen table, maybe it's the side of your bed—with a stack of bills, a phone in your hand, and that familiar knot in your stomach. You scroll through your banking app, stare at the numbers, and whisper something like, "Lord… what are we doing?"

You know how to work. You know how to hustle. You know how to survive.

But somewhere deep inside, a holy dissatisfaction has started to grow.

You're tired of wondering where your money went.

You're tired of feeling powerful in the Spirit but powerless in your finances.

You're tired of watching other communities own the buildings, the banks, the clinics, the schools—while our people do the spending but rarely the owning.

That quiet ache, that restless little voice that says, "There has to be more than this"—that's who I wrote this book for.

I did not grow up with "financial literacy." I grew up with financial survival.

I grew up hearing, "We don't have it," "Money doesn't grow on trees," "Don't ask for nothing when we go in this store." I watched adults I loved juggle overdue bills like hot coals. I saw money come in and money rush out, leaving behind exhaustion, arguments, and that familiar sigh of, "Maybe next month."

If you recognize that story, this book is for you.

You are not broken. You were simply under-taught and over-stressed. And this book is here to help change that.

Money Moves is a book about dollars, yes—but it is really a book about destiny.

It is about shifting from drifting to directing.

It is about waking up from the trance of "just getting by" and stepping into the assignment of building—for yourself, your family, and your community.

This book is also the financial literacy heartbeat of the West Philadelphia Billionaires Society (WPBS).

WPBS is a simple, radical idea:

One million people.

One dollar a day.

Moved together, on purpose, into community-owned wealth.

Not hype. Not fantasy. Math.

Imagine one million ordinary people—students, elders, single parents, entrepreneurs, church members, neighbors—each quietly moving one dollar a day into a shared vision. That's about thirty million dollars a month. Three hundred sixty-five million dollars a year.

That kind of consistent, disciplined capital can own buildings instead of just renting them. It can fund clinics, schools, banks, and businesses we don't just shop at—we own.

This book is written in that spirit.

You don't have to live in West Philadelphia to feel it. You might be in Baltimore, Detroit, Kingston, Lagos, Accra, London, Atlanta, or a small town nobody puts on the map. But if you carry the African Diaspora in your bones and you're tired of seeing our people at the bottom of every financial chart, this book is a wake-up call and a training manual rolled into one.

Here is what Money Moves will not do.

It will not shame you. It will not mock you for what you weren't taught. It will not drown you in jargon, charts, and guilt.

Here is what it will do.

It will tell you the truth—with love and a little humor.

It will speak to your conscious mind with clear teaching.

It will speak to your subconscious mind with stories, metaphors, and declarations.

It will treat you not as a victim, but as a builder in training.

You are going to hear my voices braided together in these pages.

My pastor voice, calling you higher.

My coach voice, challenging your habits.

My NLP and hypnosis trainer voice, speaking to the deeper patterns beneath your decisions.

My Christian Finance Coach voice, aligning your money with your mission.

My Deliverance Counselor voice, confronting the spiritual strongholds, lies, and generational patterns that have sat on our money for far too long.

This is not just math class. It is deliverance and discipleship for your financial life.

This is not a book to skim and forget. This is a book to work.

You will want a pen in your hand.

You will want conversations at your kitchen table.

You may have quiet moments of conviction, "aha" moments, and even a few "Lord, that's me" tears.

But you will not walk away the same if you are willing to engage.

Let me show you how we will walk this out together.

In Chapter One, you will follow the leaks. We will gently uncover where your money sneaks out at night. No more "I don't know where it goes." We pull the covers off the leaks—not to embarrass you, but to empower you.

In Chapter Two, you will confront your money stories. Every dollar you move is tied to a script in your head: "I'll always struggle." "People like us never…" "I'm just bad with money."

We expose those scripts and begin rewriting them on purpose, in line with truth instead of trauma.

In Chapter Three, you will cross a line in your identity—from consumer to owner. There is a line running through your life. On one side: "I buy." On the other side: "I build and own." We talk about stepping over that line in your mind first, then in your daily decisions.

In Chapter Four, you will learn to give every dollar a job and build your Money Map. No more wandering money. You will create a simple plan so that each dollar knows whether it is paying essentials, funding joy, building your future, or fueling community-building—including WPBS.

In Chapter Five, you will step into the One-Dollar Revolution. We dig into that "It's just a dollar" lie and flip it over. You will see how tiny, consistent moves—especially your WPBS dollar—become a quiet revolution over time, both in your life and in our communities.

In Chapter Six, we will deal with credit as a lever, not a collar. We untangle the fear and fog around credit. You will learn how to stop wearing credit like a chain around your neck and start using it as a tool, wisely and strategically, on the path to real assets.

In Chapter Seven, you will build your cushion of peace. An emergency fund is not a luxury for "other people"; it is a practical, spiritual gift you give yourself. We will build your cushion so that when life hits, you bend but do not break.

In Chapter Eight, you will begin to think in terms of many rivers, one ocean. One paycheck is too fragile. We talk about multiple streams of income that fit your gifts and your season—without idolizing hustle or sacrificing your health and soul.

In Chapter Nine, you will start writing new family wealth codes. You will learn how to teach the next generation even while you are still learning—how to change the way you talk about money in your home, and how to write new wealth "code" into your bloodline instead of passing down fear and silence.

In Chapter Ten, you will plan for more than obituaries and bills. We talk legacy—wills, insurance, beneficiaries, paperwork, and plans that keep your people from scrambling after you are gone. We will connect your personal legacy to the long-term, multi-generational vision of WPBS, so that your money decisions keep blessing people long after your name is spoken in the past tense.

You do not have to read this book like a textbook. Read it like a conversation.

Let it talk to you.

Let it step on your toes a little.

Let it encourage you a lot.

Some chapters you'll want to reread. Some sections you'll want to discuss with your spouse, your children, your church small group, your WPBS circle.

Most of all, I want you to read this as a builder, not a beggar.

You may not have grown up with wealth, but you can grow into wealth-building.

You may not have inherited assets, but you can pass them on.

You may have survived on financial fumes, but you can build a future on financial wisdom.

Take a breath, right here.

Inhale: I am not behind.

Exhale: I am beginning again, with understanding.

If you are reading this as part of a WPBS training or cohort, know that you are not alone. Thousands of others are turning these same pages, asking the same questions, making the same shifts. Your one small decision to keep reading, keep learning, and keep applying is part of a much bigger picture.

This is more than a book. It is an invitation.

To wake up.

To take your place.

To move from consumer to owner, from wandering to mapping, from random spending to Money Moves that honor God, bless your family, and help build a community we can be proud to leave behind.

Let's move.

Chapter One

Follow the Leaks: Where Your Money Sneaks Out at Night

Before we can grow your money, we have to find out where it has been escaping. Because let's be honest: for many of us, it's not that we never have money. It's that money shows up, sighs, looks around our life, and then quietly slips out the back door. By the end of the month, we're standing there saying, "I had a whole paycheck. I know I did. Where did it go?" This chapter is about following the leaks. Not to shame you. Not to embarrass you. But to wake you up in a way that is gentle, truthful, and almost funny—because when you start to see your patterns with humor, it becomes easier to change them. This is not a financial interrogation room. This is a financial awakening room. The lights are coming on. The leaks are being revealed. And you are beginning to reclaim your power.

The invisible holes in your financial bucket are what drain you. Imagine that your money is water and your life is a bucket. Every time you get paid, it's like turning on a faucet and filling that bucket. For a brief moment—on payday—you look at your bank account and you feel good. The bucket looks full. You exhale. You say, "Thank you, Lord." You might even promise yourself, "This time, I'm going to do better." But slowly, quietly, over the next few days and weeks, the water level starts dropping. Not because you made one bad decision, but because there are little holes in the bucket. Small leaks. Tiny drips. A coffee here. A fast-food run there. That subscription you forgot about. That app you signed up for during a free trial that has not been free for the last fourteen months. The "just this once" purchase that has happened about forty-seven times this year. By the time you check again, the bucket is nearly empty. You feel frustrated and confused. You say things like, "I can't get ahead," or "I'm cursed," or "I just don't make enough." And yes, income matters. But before we talk about making more, we desperately need to talk about keeping what you already have. Because if you pour more water into a bucket full of holes, all you get is faster leaks.

Your money is not judging you; it is trying to tell you a story. Right now, your bank statement is not just a list of transactions. It is a story about your habits, your fears, your desires, and your unspoken priorities. It is a diary your money has been writing about your relationship together. When you read it, you are not looking at numbers. You are looking at evidence of where your time, attention, and energy have been flowing. You are looking at patterns your conscious mind may not even notice. So in this chapter, we are going to do something radical. We are going to look—not away from your spending—but directly at it. We are going to listen—not to your excuses—but to what your money has been trying to say to you all along. Not with condemnation. With curiosity. When you approach your own financial life like a compassionate investigator instead of a harsh judge, something inside you relaxes. Your nervous system stops bracing for impact. Shame begins to loosen its grip. And the deeper part of you, the wise part, the builder in you, can begin to rise and say, "Alright. Let's tell the truth. Let's clean this up. Let's follow the leaks."

Think of this as a late-night detective story. I want you to imagine yourself as a detective—not in a trench coat and fedora, but in a t-shirt and sweatpants, sitting at your kitchen table late at night. The house is quiet. The TV is off. Your phone is facedown. It is just you, your thoughts, and your financial truth. In front of you are your bank statements, your credit card records, or your spending app, if you use one. At first, you may feel a little tension in your chest. You may feel your shoulders creep up toward your ears. You may hear that little voice saying, "I don't want to see this. I already know I'm doing bad." Take a breath. You are safe. You are not being punished. You are being awakened. As you look at the transactions, I want you to see them as clues. Each charge is a little footprint your money left behind. Coffee on Tuesday. Delivery on Wednesday. Hair, nails, lashes, barber, that "small" thing from the store that somehow became a $137 receipt. Gas. Snacks. Streaming services. Group chat trips. Random donations you made out of guilt rather than purpose. You are not judging. You are observing. You are becoming aware. Because you cannot change what you refuse to notice. And once you truly notice, you will never be able to "not know" again.

One of the biggest leaks in the bucket is what I call comfort purchases and the "I deserve it" excuse. These are the purchases you make because you are stressed, tired, bored, lonely, or angry. The money you spend to soothe your feelings instead of solving your problems. You have had a long, hard day at work. The boss was on you. The traffic was crazy. The house is loud. The world is heavy. And somewhere between the kitchen and the couch you hear a whisper inside saying, "I deserve something." That whisper does not necessarily ask, "What will help me build a better future?" It asks, "What will help me feel better right now?" You grab your phone. You open an app. You order the meal. You add something to your cart. You press the button. And for a few minutes, you feel a little better. The brain gives you a hit of satisfaction. The stress backs up a few steps. But later, when the bill comes due, you pay twice. Once with money. Once with regret. In this moment, I want you to understand something profound: you do deserve comfort. You do deserve joy. You do deserve rest, pleasure, and peace. But you also deserve a future. And your future deserves to eat too. When comfort spending becomes a pattern, it is like putting a bandage on a wound that actually needs surgery. It covers the pain temporarily but never heals the cause. So as we follow the leaks, I want you to gently notice where the phrase "I deserve it" has become an excuse to sabotage yourself. You truly do deserve better than that.

Then there is the subscription graveyard. You know exactly what I'm talking about. Somewhere in the depths of your financial life are subscriptions you forgot you had, never use, or no longer need. These are the gym memberships that only your bank account visits, the apps you downloaded for a free trial, the streaming services you signed up for because of one show three years ago. Each one is small. Eight dollars here. Twelve dollars there. Five dollars over there. Nothing seems catastrophic. But together, they start to make a noise. It's like having tiny little financial mosquitoes buzzing around your head. Individually, they are just annoying. Collectively, they drain you. If you could see your subscriptions gather in a room, some would be standing there looking guilty, shuffling their feet, saying, "We know. We know. We've been taking your money and giving you nothing in return." They might even apologize if you gave them the chance. And the beautiful thing is: you can give them that chance. You can say, with authority and love for yourself, "This is the month I clean the graveyard. This is the month I cancel what does not serve me." You are not being mean. You are being a good steward. You are honoring the future you are building.

The silent partner you forgot is your future self. Every dollar you spend is a conversation between your present self and your future self. But for most of us, the future self does not get a vote. The present self is loud. The present self says, "I want it now. I want it delivered. I don't want to wait. I don't want to think. I'm tired. I deserve this." Meanwhile, your future self is standing there in the corner, like a quiet partner in the business of your life, raising their hand and saying, "Um… excuse me. If you spend all of that now, what exactly am I supposed to live on?" Your future self is the person you will be at sixty, seventy, eighty years old. They are the one who will either say, "I'm grateful you made those sacrifices and those shifts," or "I wish you had taken this more seriously when you had the chance." In this chapter, as we follow the leaks, I want you to start thinking of your future self as a real person. Picture them. Imagine their face. See where they live. See how they feel. Do they wake up with peace in their heart or anxiety in their chest? Do they walk into a home they own or a place they're scrambling to afford? Are they still working when they are exhausted, or are they choosing how they spend their time? When you look at your spending, ask, "Did I consult my future self? Or did I leave them out of the meeting?" The more you learn to honor your future self, the less willing you become to tolerate unnecessary leaks in the present.

Now let's talk about the WPBS angle: leaks don't just hurt you—they hurt the vision. This is bigger than you. This is bigger than one paycheck, one bill, one month of frustration. Every unnecessary leak in your life is not just money lost—it is power lost. It is opportunity lost. It is one more delay in the timeline of community transformation. Think of it this way: every time you patch a leak, you are not just helping yourself. You are freeing up dollars that can be aimed, like arrows, toward purpose. Toward paying down debt. Toward building savings. Toward investing. Toward supporting the WPBS movement and the kind of community-owned assets that change neighborhoods forever. When a million people find and plug their leaks, that is not just personal progress. That is a quiet revolution. The enemy of your future wants your resources scattered, distracted, emotional, and disorganized. God wants your resources focused, purposeful, and aligned. WPBS gives us a vision big enough to say, "My little leak is not so little after all. My one dollar, my ten dollars, my fifty dollars—when directed with wisdom—are part of something historic." As you follow your leaks, know this: every dollar you save from waste becomes a soldier in the army of your assignment.

I call this next part a gentle X-ray: a simple first exercise. Let's make this extremely practical. I want you to pick a recent month of your spending. Not your "best behavior" month where you tried hard, and not your "worst disaster" month where everything collapsed. Just an ordinary month. In that month, look at every transaction and gently, compassionately, place it into one of a few mental categories: "must have," "nice to have," and "leaks." Must-haves are the basic essentials of life: rent or mortgage, utilities, basic groceries, necessary transportation, basic insurance. Nice-to-haves are things that add joy and convenience but are not essential: outings, entertainment, extras, some subscriptions. Leaks are what you know in your spirit are not truly serving you or your future: impulse buys, comfort spending, unused subscriptions, duplicate services, charges you don't even recognize. You do not have to write this down in this moment if you're just reading, but as you imagine this exercise, you can feel something beginning to organize inside you. Your mind is quietly sorting. "Yes, that's a must. That's nice. That, right there—that's a leak." Notice how, just by mentally naming it, the leak loses some of its power. Because awareness is the first move of transformation.

From this point forward, no more "I don't know where it goes." One of the most common sentences people say about their money is, "I don't know where it goes." That sentence is a spell. It hypnotizes you into helplessness. It tells your brain, "We are not in control." It tells your future, "We're just going to drift." In this chapter, I want you to break that spell. From this day forward, you never again say, "I don't know where it goes," without quickly correcting yourself. If the words slip out, catch them and replace them with, "I am learning exactly where it goes, and I am directing it on purpose." That one shift in language begins to rewire your nervous system. Even before every habit changes, your identity is changing. You are moving from passive victim of your finances to active steward of your resources. Say this right now, even if only in your mind: "I am learning where my money goes. I am following the leaks. I am taking my power back." You may notice a calm seriousness rising in you as you say it. That is you waking up.

I want to tell you the story of "just five dollars." Imagine a person who says, "It's just five dollars." They say it about coffee. About snacks. About that extra streaming channel. About a small in-app purchase. About a lottery ticket. Nothing wrong, nothing evil, just "small." But they say it ten times in a week. That's fifty dollars. They say it forty-five times in a month. That's two hundred twenty-five dollars. They say it hundreds of times over the course of a year. Now we're talking thousands. "Just five dollars" becomes a quiet thief. Not loud, not dramatic, just consistent. Meanwhile, that same person says, "I don't have money to save. I don't have money to invest. I don't have money to support WPBS. I don't have money to build anything." But the truth is not that they don't have money. The truth is that "just five dollars" has been running the show. When you begin to follow the leaks, "just five dollars" gets exposed. You start to see that small amounts, aimed correctly, are powerful. And small amounts, leaked carelessly, are dangerous. From now on, when you feel "It's just…" rising on your tongue, you can pause and ask, "What if this 'just' could become part of something greater?" Again, this is not about deprivation. This is about awareness. There will be times you say, "Yes, I will spend this five, ten, or twenty and enjoy it fully." The difference is: it will be a conscious choice, not an unconscious leak.

Every leak you identify is not a reason to feel ashamed; it is a revelation of leadership. You are discovering where you can lead yourself better. Think of a great leader you admire. They do not become great because they never make mistakes. They become great because they pay attention, course-correct, and learn. In the same way, you are now becoming the leader of your money rather than its follower. As you walk through your spending, you may find areas that feel tender. You may see a pattern of eating out when you feel lonely. You may notice you shop more when you feel rejected. You may realize you give money away impulsively to avoid saying no, then later struggle to pay your own bills. Instead of beating yourself up, I want you to say, "Thank you,

Lord, for showing me this. Now that I see it, I can heal it. I can grow. I can change." You are not just plugging financial leaks. You are healing emotional wounds. You are learning new ways to comfort yourself that don't destroy your future. You are stepping into mature stewardship. And as you do, you are becoming a living example—a walking testimony—for your family, your friends, and your community. You are becoming someone who can say, "I used to be completely lost with money. But I followed the leaks. I learned the patterns. I changed. And if I can change, you can too." That is leadership.

From leaks to flow—that is the journey. As you complete this chapter, something subtle yet powerful may already be happening. You might feel more curious about your own numbers. You might feel less afraid to look. You might sense that this, right here, is a turning point. Follow that feeling. From this point on, imagine your money not as a chaotic spray of random spending, but as a flowing river. Your job is to shape the riverbanks. To redirect the flow away from the leaks and toward the things that matter: your stability, your dignity, your dreams, your family, your community, and the WPBS vision of community-owned wealth. Every leak you patch strengthens the flow. Every leak you close frees more power. Every leak you expose and heal brings you one step closer to the life you are designed to live. Take another breath. You are waking up. Your money is waking up. And together, you are beginning to move in a new direction. In the chapters that follow, we will build on this awareness. We will transform your newfound clarity into practical strategy—budgeting with purpose, saving with ease, using credit as a tool, and investing in ways that make sense for you and for the movement. But all of that begins here, with this simple, courageous act: you have decided to follow the leaks. And because you have decided, things are already changing.

Money Stories: The Scripts in Your Head That Keep You Broke or Make You Brave

Before your bank account ever moved, your mind did. Long before a dollar left your hand, a belief whispered in your ear. Before you ever made a purchase, signed a loan, swiped a card, or said, "I can't afford that," a story was already playing inside you. That story is your money script. And like an actor on stage, you have been repeating your lines so long you may have forgotten they were not written by you.

This chapter is about those stories. The quiet sentences that slide through your mind when you see a price tag, hear about an opportunity, or dream about something bigger. "We don't have it." "People like us don't get ahead." "It's always something." "I'm just trying to survive." On the other side, there are different scripts: "I can learn this." "God will give me wisdom." "I am a builder." "I can be trusted with more." Both sets of sentences are like seeds. And your financial life, right now, is a garden growing from what you've been planting.

None of this is about blame. You didn't wake up one morning and say, "Let me choose the most self-sabotaging script possible." Most of your money stories were inherited. You caught them, like a cold, from the environment you grew up in. You heard them at the kitchen table, in the living room, standing in line at the store, sitting in church, watching TV, listening to music. They seeped in through repetition and emotion, until they felt like "just the way life is." In this chapter, we are not here to condemn those voices. We are here to become aware of them, bless the ones that helped us survive, and consciously retire the ones that no longer serve the life God is calling us to build.

I want you to imagine your money stories as a choir. Some voices are singing faith, vision, and wisdom: "We can figure this out. There is a way. Let's learn, let's grow, let's plan." Other voices are singing fear, scarcity, and resignation: "What's the use? It never works out. Don't even try." Whichever section of the choir you turn the microphone toward will dominate your life's soundtrack. Our work in this chapter is not to pretend the fearful voices don't exist; it is to recognize them, turn their volume down, and deliberately turn the volume up on the voices that sing of possibility, stewardship, and abundance.

Think back to your childhood for a moment. When did you first notice money? Maybe it was when you saw your parents arguing over a bill. Maybe it was when you wanted something in a store and heard, "Put that back, we don't have it." Maybe it was when the lights got cut off, or when the rent was late, or when you overheard grown folks whispering about "how tight things are right now." Those moments are not just memories; they are roots. Your nervous system remembers the tension, the embarrassment, the fear, the shame, and the quiet vows you made: "When I grow up, I'll never…" or "I guess this is just how it is for us."

Some of those vows turned you into a hustler—driven, hardworking, always pushing. Others turned you into an avoider—tired, overwhelmed, distancing yourself from anything that feels like "too much." Both reactions are understandable. Both were forms of self-protection. But now, as an adult, as someone reading a book like this, as someone called to build and to own and to participate in the WPBS vision, it's time to ask a powerful, loving question: "Are my old survival stories still running my life? Or am I ready to write something new?"

Let's talk about one very common story: "We're just not those kind of people." Those kind of people might be homeowners, investors, entrepreneurs, or "rich folks." If you grew up seeing wealth as something other people had—other neighborhoods, other families, other skin tones—you may have unconsciously accepted the role of an outsider. Money, in your mind, might feel like a party you were never invited to. So when you hear about owning a business, buying property, building a portfolio, or participating in community ownership like WPBS, your first reaction isn't excitement; it's suspicion. "That's for them, not us. That's for people who already have money. That's for people who grew up with it."

Here's the truth: there is no such thing as "those kind of people" born with a special money gene. There are only people who have learned certain skills, adopted certain habits, and rehearsed certain stories long enough that they became normal. The good news is, stories can be changed, and skills can be learned. The moment you say, "Maybe I can be one of those people who own things, who build things, who invest, who leave something behind," your brain opens a new file. It starts searching for ways to make that statement true. That's how powerful your words and inner stories are.

Another common script goes like this: "Money is the root of all evil." You may have heard it quoted that way so many times that you never questioned it. But the actual Scripture says, "The love of money is the root of all kinds of evil." The obsession, the worship, the greed, the willingness to hurt others to get it—that's the problem. Money itself is a tool. In the hands of the wicked, it builds systems of oppression, exploitation, and harm. In the hands of the righteous, it builds schools, clinics, safe housing, healthy food systems, kingdom work, and generational stability. If you secretly believe that wanting more money automatically makes you "less spiritual," you will sabotage yourself every time you start to gain momentum.

If that script lives in you, it may sound something like this: "If I get too successful, I might turn into one of those greedy people. Better stay humble. Better stay small." So you undercharge, you overgive, you never ask for a raise, you feel guilty when you save or invest. You give away what you need to keep. You confuse poverty with holiness, and struggle with righteousness. Family, that is not God. That is a twisted script. The God who owns the cattle on a thousand hills is not threatened by you having enough. He is not intimidated by you becoming a good steward of more. What He resists is pride, arrogance, injustice, and systems that crush the poor.

Now imagine this: instead of "Money is evil," your new script becomes, "Money is a servant in my life, not my master." Feel the difference. "Money is a tool in my assignment." "Money in my hands will fund good things." "I do not chase money; I attract it through wisdom, service, and alignment, and I deploy it according to God's heart." As you sit with those statements, you may notice a shift, even now. Your shoulders might drop. Your breathing might deepen. The internal war between "I want more" and "I shouldn't want more" begins to calm down. When that internal war quiets, you can finally think clearly, plan wisely, and act boldly.

There is another story many of us carry: "I'm just bad with money." It sounds innocent, almost funny—like a personality quirk. "I can't do numbers. I'm terrible with money." You might even say it with a laugh, like a joke you tell on yourself. But your subconscious mind does not treat it as a joke. It treats it as a command. If you declare, over and over, "I'm bad with money," your brain will not bother trying to get good. Why should it? You've already made the decision. That story becomes a self-fulfilling prophecy. You avoid learning. You avoid asking questions. You avoid looking at the numbers. You feel childish and ashamed, so you stay confused.

What if you shifted that script just a little? Instead of "I'm bad with money," try, "No one ever taught me about money, but I am learning now." Do you feel the difference? The first script is a sentence. The second script is a journey. The first shuts you down. The second opens you up. When you say, "I am learning," you give yourself permission to be a beginner. Beginners are allowed to ask questions. Beginners are allowed to make mistakes and keep going. Beginners are allowed to grow. Every financially wise person you admire was once a beginner who didn't know what they were doing. They chose learning over shame. You can make that same choice.

Your family history also plays a huge role in your money stories. Maybe you come from a line of people who scraped by, stretched every dollar, and made miracles with very little. You learned resilience and creativity, the art of "making a way out of no way." That is a gift. At the same time, you may have also learned constant anxiety, chronic scarcity thinking, and the belief that "there's never enough," even when there is. On the other hand, you might have grown up around people who spent freely whenever money showed up, because there was no expectation it would be there tomorrow. "Live it up while you can" was the unspoken rule. That, too, is a story.

In this moment, I want you to picture yourself standing between your ancestors and your descendants. Behind you are generations who survived racism, exploitation, redlining, layoffs, unfair wages, denied loans, broken promises, and systemic obstruction. They did the best they could with what they had. In front of you are generations yet unborn, who will inherit either your patterns or your growth. You are the bridge. You are the pattern breaker. You are the one saying, "Thank you for what you taught me about surviving. I honor you. And now I choose to learn how to build, own, and thrive so that those coming after me don't have to start from scratch."

You are not dishonoring your family by wanting to do better. You are fulfilling their deepest prayers. Many of them said with weary voices, "I just want my children to have it better than I did." When you heal your money stories, you are answering that prayer. You are taking the baton and running a new leg of the race. You are moving from "We get by" to "We build." From "We rent" to "We own." From "We hope somebody helps us" to "We are the somebody, and we are helping ourselves and each other."

Now, let's bring WPBS into the picture. One of the most dangerous stories we've been fed is that our community is permanently poor, permanently behind, permanently dependent. That we are "bad with money" as a people. That we cannot organize, cannot sustain, cannot manage large amounts, cannot run institutions. That story has been told about us loudly and repeatedly. And if we are not careful, we will repeat it ourselves, reinforcing the very chains we are trying to break. WPBS says, "No. That is not who we are." WPBS says, "We have always built. We have always created. We have always been resourceful. What we lacked was not capacity, but coordinated ownership."

When you change your personal money story from "I'm just trying to make it" to "I am a builder and a stakeholder," you become spiritually and mentally capable of participating in something like WPBS. You stop seeing yourself as a desperate individual grabbing for crumbs and start seeing yourself as part of a collective table-building project. Your inner voice shifts from "I'm broke, what's one dollar?" to "I am powerful, and my consistent contributions—both to my own goals and to our shared vision—matter." That inner shift is what transforms WPBS from a nice idea into a living, breathing movement.

So how do you actually change a money story? This is where we slip into a little mental rehearsal, a little sanctified self-hypnosis, a little Scriptural renewal of the mind. First, you become aware of the old script. Catch it. Hear it. Don't rush past it. When you feel yourself saying, "I'll never get out of debt," pause. When you hear, "People like us don't own businesses," pause. When "It's always something" rises up, pause. In that pause, you breathe and you ask, "Is this story absolutely true? Or is this just the story I have rehearsed?"

Second, you offer yourself a new, better story that is believable, hopeful, and aligned with where you're going. Not a fake, sugary affirmation you don't believe, but a bridge statement. Instead of "I'll never get out of debt," you say, "I am learning how to get out of debt, step by step." Instead of "People like us don't own businesses," you say, "More and more people like us are starting to own things, and I can be one of them." Instead of "It's always something," you say, "I am learning to build margin and resilience, so when something happens, I am ready."

As you repeat these new statements, slowly, thoughtfully, with feeling, you are rewiring your inner script. Your brain is plastic—it can change. Neurons that used to fire together in fear, despair, and avoidance can begin to fire together in faith, strategy, and action. The key is repetition with emotion. Scripture calls it meditating day and night—turning truth over and over in your mind until it becomes part of you. You are doing the same with your new money stories.

Third, you take actions, however small, that agree with your new story. If your new story is, "I am learning how to manage money wisely," then you might watch one financial literacy video, read one article, open one savings account, or track your spending for one week. If your new story is, "I can be an owner," you might start by researching how to open a business, support a Black-owned business, or participate in a community investment initiative like WPBS. Every small action is like underlining the new script in your mind. You are proving to yourself that you mean it.

Here's a simple exercise you can begin to practice. Imagine your "Old Money Story" sitting in a chair on your left. It might look tired, anxious, hunched over. It might sound like, "We never have enough," "I'm always behind," "Money is hard for me." On your right, picture your "New Money Story" sitting in another chair.

This version of you is calmer, more focused, more hopeful. They say things like, "I am learning," "I am growing," "I am trusted with resources," "I am part of something big."

Now, close your eyes and mentally step from the left chair to the right. Feel the difference in your body. The way you breathe. The way you sit. The way you look at the future. Let yourself sit there for a few moments. Let that version of you look back at the old version and say, with compassion, "Thank you for trying to protect me. Thank you for surviving. But I've got it from here. We are safe enough now to build." This is not just imagination; this is neurological rehearsal. You are practicing being the new you, so that when you make real-world decisions, that version of you shows up more quickly.

Sometimes, your old money story will use spiritual language to keep you stuck. It will say, "Just wait on the Lord" when God has already given you clarity and opportunity. It will shrug and say, "If God wants me to have it, He will drop it in my lap," while you scroll your phone and ignore the resources, trainings, and plans right in front of you. Faith is not passive. The same Bible that says trust God also says, "Be diligent," "Count the cost," "Be faithful over a few things," "Write the vision and make it plain." Your new story holds faith and wisdom together. "God is my Source, and I am a wise steward. I pray, and I plan. I believe, and I budget. I sow, and I also learn about soil, water, and harvest."

Let's also be honest: some of our money stories are laced with trauma. If you've ever had a car repossessed, an eviction notice on the door, a foreclosure, wage garnishment, or bankruptcy, those events carry weight. They can leave emotional bruises. So every time you think about finances, your body flinches. Your heart speeds up. You avoid, because looking at money feels like walking back into a painful memory. If that's you, I want you to hear this: your past mistakes and crises do not disqualify you from financial wisdom; they qualify you. You know what it feels like to fall. You know the sting. Now you are learning what it feels like to rise.

Can you imagine a future version of you speaking to someone else who is where you used to be? Picture yourself, a few years from now, sitting across from a friend, a niece, a nephew, a client, saying, "I know what it's like to be overwhelmed by debt. I know what it is to feel like you'll never catch up. I've been there. But let me tell you what I learned. Let me tell you how I changed my story. Let me show you how God and wisdom walked me out of that mess." Feel the authority in that. That is not theoretical. That is lived testimony. Your new money story is not just for you; it is for every person you will touch.

Now bring this down to a very simple, very present moment. As you read this chapter, notice the stories trying to pop up right now. Maybe one says, "This sounds good, but my situation is different." Another says, "I've heard all this before; I never stick with it." Another says, "You're too old to change now," or "You've messed up too much." Catch those thoughts. Don't let them slip by unquestioned. They are old scripts defending their territory. Smile at them and say, "I hear you. You've been with me a long time. But we're doing something different now."

Then gently introduce a new story: "Even now, I can learn something that changes my life." "Even now, God can give me wisdom and strength." "Even now, my small consistent changes can create a big difference over time." "Even now, I can participate in building wealth for myself, my family, and my community."

Money Stories: The Scripts in Your Head that Keep You Broke
or Make You Brave

Your old story says, "It's too late." Your new story says, "It's right on time." Which one will you give your agreement to?

As you continue through this book, you are not just absorbing information; you are undergoing a quiet rewiring. You may notice yourself speaking differently, even in casual conversation. You might catch yourself before saying, "I'm so broke," and instead say, "My money is tight right now, but I'm learning how to direct it better." You might stop calling yourself "horrible with money" and start saying, "I'm becoming more disciplined." These may seem like small changes, but remember: stories are seeds. Words are containers. What you speak over yourself shapes how you see, and how you see shapes how you act.

You are not alone in this process. As you shift your money stories, others around you will feel it. Some will be inspired and want to join you. Some will be uncomfortable, because your change challenges their comfort. That's okay. You are not responsible for maintaining everyone else's familiar patterns. You are responsible for answering the call on your own life. As you align your financial stories with truth, wisdom, and purpose, you will naturally attract people, tools, and opportunities that match that alignment. You will also gently outgrow relationships and environments that demand you stay small, scared, and stuck.

In WPBS, we are not simply asking people to put in a dollar a day. We are inviting them into a new identity: citizen-owner, builder, stakeholder. That identity must be supported by new stories. "I'm not just paying bills; I'm building assets." "I'm not just working for money; I'm learning to make money work for me and for us." "I'm not just reacting to emergencies; I'm preparing for opportunities." These are the kinds of statements that support a movement, not just an individual budget.

As we move to the next chapter, I want you to carry this simple practice with you: when you feel fear, scarcity, or shame rise up around money, pause and ask, "What story am I telling myself right now?" Name it. Then ask, "What story do I choose instead?" Speak that new story out loud if you can. Whisper it if you must. Write it in your journal. Put it on a sticky note. Put it in your phone. Let it echo in your mind when you wake up and when you go to sleep. Over time, those chosen stories will become your default, and your financial decisions will begin to line up with the new script.

You are not the sum of your past mistakes. You are not the echo of other people's fears. You are not trapped in the stories you were handed as a child. You are a grown, gifted, called, anointed, learning, evolving person who can choose new thoughts, new beliefs, and new behaviors. You are a builder in training. A steward in formation. A WPBS Billionaire-in-Training rewriting the narrative for yourself, your family, and your community.

Take a deep breath and let that sink in. Your money story is not fixed. It is a living, editable script. With God's help, with wisdom, with practice, and with community, you are turning the page. In the chapters ahead, we will take these new stories and anchor them in practical habits—budgeting, saving, using credit wisely, and positioning yourself to own instead of only renting. But for now, know this: the most important construction site in your financial life is not your wallet; it is your mind. And right now, as you read, the renovation has already begun.

Chapter Three

From Consumer to Owner: Stepping Across the Line

There is a line running through your life that you may not have known was there. On one side of that line is the consumer. On the other side is the owner. Most of us were born on the consumer side. We were trained, marketed to, and conditioned to stay there. We've been taught to be excellent customers, loyal subscribers, faithful buyers, and dependable bill payers. But very few of us were ever trained to cross that line and say, "Wait a minute… I don't just want to buy things from the table. I want to own the table. I want to help build the restaurant. I want a piece of the block, not just a receipt from the corner store." This chapter is about that line. It is about the moment you look down at your own feet and say, "Today, I am stepping over."

Being a consumer is not evil. We all consume. We need food, clothing, shelter, transportation, and some joy along the way. The problem is not that we consume; the problem is when

31

consumption becomes our entire identity. When the only role we know how to play in the economy is "the one who spends." When we measure our worth by what we wear, drive, or carry in our hand, instead of what we build, own, and leave. When every paycheck passes through our hands on its way to somebody else's balance sheet, and we never stop to ask, "Where do I appear in this picture as an owner?"

Think about your day from morning to night. You wake up in a bed someone else manufactured, in a home you might be renting or paying a mortgage on. You check a phone made by a company whose stock price rises when you upgrade. You scroll on platforms that make money from your attention. You drink coffee or tea from a brand that has its own shareholders. You get in a car manufactured by another corporation, drive on roads you help pay for, and go to work to help someone else's organization grow. Almost every moment of your day, someone owns something that you are paying to use. The question is not, "Is this wrong?" The question is, "Where in this entire chain does my ownership show up?"

For many of us, the answer has been, "Nowhere." Not because we're lazy, not because we're unintelligent, but because we were never invited into that side of the conversation. Growing up, you might have heard, "Pay your bills on time," but you probably didn't hear, "Let's talk about equity, shares, and community ownership." You may have learned how to apply for a job, but no one sat you down and said, "Here is how you buy a piece of the company. Here is how you become a landlord, not just a tenant. Here is how you and your neighbors could own this block together." Instead, the world ran a 24/7 commercial in your mind: "Buy. Consume. Impress. Keep up."

There is a subtle language difference that reveals where you stand. Consumers say, "I love this brand." Owners say, "I own this brand." Consumers say, "They raised the prices again." Owners say, "Our revenue just went up; how are we reinvesting?" Consumers stand in line outside the store on release day. Owners sit in meetings deciding what the store will sell. Consumers get the bag. Owners get the profit. I'm not demonizing the bag—enjoy your shoes, your phone, your food. But I want you to recognize that there is a seat with your name on it at a different level of the table. And every step you take in this chapter is you moving closer to that seat.

Let's talk identity for a moment. When you hear the word "owner," who do you see in your mind? Do you picture someone who looks like you, from a neighborhood like yours, with a story like yours? Or do you picture someone far away—wealthy, distant, faceless, living behind gates and tinted windows? If your inner picture of ownership doesn't include people who look, sound, and move like you, then your subconscious will treat ownership as something foreign. It will whisper, "That's not us. That's them." And as long as your mind says "that's them," your feet won't move toward it.

One of the most powerful things you can do is rewrite that picture. Begin to see "owner" with your face on it. See "landlord," "shareholder," "business partner," "co-op member," with your hands, your voice, your story. Imagine walking down a street and saying, "Our people own that building, that shop, that clinic, that bank." Not as a fantasy, but as a living reality. WPBS is an invitation to make that picture real, not just for a few, but for many. It is an invitation to say, "We will not be permanent renters in a world our ancestors helped build. We will be owners."

There is a mindset shift that has to happen for this to be possible. Consumers ask, "How can I get this now?" Owners ask, "How does this pay me later?" Consumers focus on price. Owners focus on value. Consumers ask, "How much does it cost per month?" Owners ask, "What is the return over years?" Consumers say, "I deserve this purchase." Owners say, "I deserve the security, freedom, and influence that comes from owning assets." Notice how both sides talk about deserving. Both want something. The difference is the time horizon. One is reaching for quick satisfaction; the other is reaching for long-term strength.

You may think, "But I don't have enough to be an owner. I barely have enough to make it." That is the old story talking. Ownership is not just about having huge sums of money. It is about direction. It starts in tiny, almost invisible ways. The first time you choose to put ten dollars into savings instead of into a fast-food order you don't really want, you just practiced ownership. The first time you set aside a small amount for investing, even if it's through a simple app or workplace plan, you stepped over the line. The first time you say, "No, I'm not buying that now. I'm building something," you crossed an invisible border in your spirit.

Ownership also begins with questions. When you hand your money to a company, ask yourself, "Do I own any piece of this, even indirectly?" When you see a building you love, ask, "Who owns this? Is there a path, even a small one, for me or my community to own something like this?" When people in your community start a business, ask, "How can I support this so it grows and stays in our hands?" You may not be able to answer all those questions today, but asking them wakes up something inside you. It shifts you from passive to active, from "life happens to me" to "I participate in shaping my life and my community."

From Consumer to Owner: Stepping Across the Line

Let me share a simple picture. Imagine two people receiving the exact same paycheck. The first spends all of it on bills, food, transportation, entertainment, and impulse buys. Honest, real needs. A few wants. At the end of the month, they have memories, receipts, and maybe a lingering feeling of, "Where did it all go?" The second person, with the same income, does something different. They pay the essentials. They enjoy some wants. But they also decide that a small percentage of their money—maybe five percent at first, maybe ten—is going toward ownership. That money goes into savings, investments, and eventually into shared ventures and community projects like WPBS. Five years later, their incomes may still be similar on paper, but one has assets and options growing quietly in the background. The other has only bills and stories about how hard life is. The difference started with a decision: "Some of this money must start working for me and for us."

Stepping from consumer to owner will sometimes feel like swimming against the current. The whole world is designed to keep you consuming. Your phone is full of ads. Your email is full of offers. Your social media feed is full of beautiful things you didn't know you needed until thirty seconds ago. You will have moments where the pull to buy, upgrade, and impress feels strong. In those moments, I want you to hear a new inner voice rising—a voice that sounds like the owner version of you. It says, "I see that. It's nice. But right now, I'm more interested in building than in flexing." Sometimes you will buy the thing; sometimes you will walk away. The power is in knowing you have a choice, and in choosing ownership often enough that it becomes a habit.

On a deeper level, moving from consumer to owner is also about healing how you see yourself. If you have been told for years that you are "behind," "less than," "not good with money," "always struggling," those labels can bury your true identity. Ownership begins with a quiet declaration: "I am worthy of owning things. I am capable of learning what I need to know. I am allowed to have stability, not just survival. I am allowed to leave something behind." When that declaration takes root, your behavior slowly follows. You don't have to be perfect. You just have to be consistent.

Think about how WPBS shifts this conversation. Alone, you may feel like your small ownership efforts are insignificant. "What difference does my tiny investment make?" But in a movement like WPBS, your small ownership effort is multiplied by thousands, then hundreds of thousands, then a million participants. Your dollar a day, your financial discipline, your decision to own instead of only consume, becomes part of a collective engine. That engine can fund businesses we control, purchase properties we decide over, and build institutions our children inherit. When you step from consumer to owner personally, you also step from spectator to partner in WPBS. You are not just reading about the vision; you are resourcing the vision.

You might be thinking, "That sounds amazing, but where do I even start?" Start where you are, with what you have, right now. If all you can do this month is open a savings account and put something in it, do that. If you can research a beginner-friendly way to invest a small amount, do that. If you can support a Black-owned business, do that. If you can set up your dollar-a-day commitment to WPBS as part of your giving and investing plan, do that. Each of these steps is like placing a brick on the owner's side of the line. Over time, those bricks become a foundation.

Notice how this feels in your body as you read. When you think, "I am an owner in training," does your chest expand a little? Do you sit up a bit straighter? When you imagine your name on a deed, a share, a partnership agreement, does something hopeful move in your spirit? That is your inner owner waking up. Let that feeling grow. Let it challenge your old doubts and insecurities. Let it remind you that you are not just at the mercy of bills and prices. You are a participant in something bigger.

At the same time, be gentle with yourself. Crossing this line will bring up resistance. There will be days you slip back into old patterns, buying to numb pain or impress people who don't matter. There will be moments you feel overwhelmed by information. There will be voices around you, and sometimes inside you, saying, "You're doing too much. Just live your life." In those moments, remember why you started. Remember the elder on the couch saying, "If I had known then what I know now…" Remember the children and grandchildren who will live in the world you help build. Remember the streets you want to see lined with businesses that say, "Community-Owned" instead of "Closed" or "Under New Management" by someone who doesn't live there.

Stepping into ownership is not about becoming obsessed with money. It is about becoming responsible with purpose. It is about saying, "I will not let my entire life's work vanish into other people's pockets without leaving a trace for those I love and the community I come from." It is about aligning your finances with your faith, your values, and your calling. When you see money as a tool in God's hands, working through your hands, ownership becomes an act of worship and stewardship, not greed.

Imagine a future version of you, maybe ten years from now, standing in front of a building with a small group of young people. They're listening as you say, "You see this place? I own a piece of this. Our community owns a piece of this. I remember when all I did was pay bills and hope I could make it to the next paycheck. But then I started to follow the leaks. I changed my stories. I stepped from consumer to owner. It started small, but I kept going. And now I can show you how to do the same." That moment is not out of reach. It is on the other side of many small, faithful steps that begin right here, right now.

As we prepare to move into the next chapter, I want you to hold onto a simple phrase: "I buy some things, but I own other things." Say it slowly. Let it sink in. Today, it might be mostly a statement of faith. Over time, it will become a statement of fact. You may start by owning small amounts—modest savings, beginner investments, participation in community projects. But small ownership is still ownership. It carries a different energy than pure consumption. It sends a different message to your brain, your spirit, and your lineage.

You are crossing a line in this chapter. Not with fireworks or loud announcements, but with a quiet inner decision that will echo for years. You are no longer just a consumer waiting for the next sale, the next opportunity to spend. You are an owner-in-development, a builder in formation, a WPBS Billionaire-in-Training learning to direct your money toward assets, not just appetites. Take a deep breath and feel the ground under your feet. The line is behind you now. You have stepped across.

In the chapters to come, we will get even more practical—talking about how to organize your money so ownership becomes automatic, how to build an emergency cushion, how to use credit as a lever instead of a collar, and how to position yourself to invest wisely. But all of those strategies rest on this inner shift. Consumer to owner. Spectator to stakeholder. Customer to co-creator. You have begun that shift. And because you have, the way you see every dollar from this day forward will never be the same.

Chapter Four

Give Every Dollar a Job: Building Your Money Map

By now, you have started following the leaks. You have begun to change your money stories. You have stepped—at least in your heart—from pure consumer to budding owner. That alone is powerful. But without a simple, practical plan, your money will still wander. It doesn't matter how inspired you feel on Sunday if, by Friday, your dollars are once again out in the world freeloading with no assignment. Inspiration without direction leads right back to, "I had money… I just don't know where it went." In this chapter, we are going to fix that. We are going to give every dollar a job. We are going to build your Money Map.

A Money Map is not a punishment. It is not a financial prison. It is not some angry, joyless document that tells you "no" all the time. A Money Map is simply a written version of you being in charge. It is you telling your money, "Here is where you go. Here is what you do. Here is how you serve my life, my future, my family, and my community." Without that map, your money makes its own plans. And usually, your money's "plans" involve disappearing into impulse buys, random fees, and other people's dreams. With a map, you move from reaction to intention. You stop being surprised by your own spending, and you start being strategic.

Some people hear the word "budget" and feel a knot form in their stomach. Maybe you've tried before and felt like you failed. Maybe you associate budgeting with scarcity, deprivation, or arguments. So instead of using a word that triggers old stress, I want you to think "Money Map." A map is something you create when you're going somewhere. It's not a list of what you can't do; it's a guide to help you get where you want to go without getting lost. That's exactly what this chapter is about: helping you stop getting lost with your money.

Imagine you are the CEO of You, Inc. Every month, a certain amount of money walks into your office in the form of your income. Each dollar is like a new employee on your team, standing there waiting for instructions. Some of those dollars are saying, "Put me toward the light bill." Others are saying, "Assign me to groceries, transportation, rent." Others could be assigned to savings, debt payoff, investing, giving, and supporting WPBS. The worst thing you can do as CEO is shrug and say, "Just wander around and see what happens." If you ran an organization that way, it would collapse. Yet many of us have been running our financial life exactly like that—no clear roles, no defined priorities, just chaos and vibes.

Giving every dollar a job is you stepping into your CEO role. It is you saying, "From now on, we don't do random. We do purpose." It doesn't mean you will never have surprises. Life happens. Tires go flat. Kids outgrow shoes in two weeks. Friends get married. Bodies get sick. Emergencies show up uninvited. But when you have a Money Map, even the surprises land differently. You have a framework. You have a way to pivot. You are not just getting hit; you are responding.

Let's keep this simple. A basic Money Map starts with three big categories: what must be paid, what supports your joy and quality of life, and what builds your future. That's it. Must-be-paid are your essentials: housing, utilities, basic food, transportation, minimum debt payments, basic insurance. Joy and quality-of-life spending includes outings, entertainment, eating out, hair, nails, giving gifts, small pleasures that make life feel human and not like a spreadsheet. Future-building includes savings, emergency fund, investing, extra debt paydown, and contributions to movements like WPBS that create long-term community wealth. Every dollar you receive belongs in one of those three destinations.

Right now, without even seeing your numbers, we already know what tends to happen. Most of the money goes to must-be-paid and joy now, and very little goes to future-building. It's not because you don't care about the future; it's because the present screams louder. Bills scream. Kids scream. Cravings scream. Ads scream. By the time you think about the future, there is nothing left to send. Your Money Map is how you flip that script. You don't starve the present, but you stop letting it bully the future. You decide—before the month begins—what percentage of your money will be devoted to each purpose.

You might be thinking, "That sounds great, but my money is already spoken for." I hear you. But I want you to consider something: even if your income is tight, you still make choices. You still decide who gets paid first, whether the fast-food drive-thru gets your last thirty dollars, or whether your emergency fund does. You still decide whether your future self gets anything at all. A Money Map doesn't magically increase your income. It increases your clarity. It takes your scattered, unconscious decisions and brings them into the light where you can see them, adjust them, and over time, improve them.

Here's a gentle way to begin. Take your typical monthly income—whether it's from a job, business, benefits, or a mix—and write that number at the top of a page. Then list your essentials with honest monthly amounts. You don't have to make it perfect; this is not an exam. Just get it down: housing, utilities, basic groceries, transportation, minimum payments, basic phone, basic internet, essential insurance. Subtract that total from your income. What's left is what you've been spending on everything else, usually without a plan. That "everything else" is where leaks, comfort spending, and future-building wrestle each other every month.

Now, rather than letting that leftover just disappear, we will pre-decide. You might say, "Out of what's left, this percentage goes to joy, and this percentage goes to the future." Maybe at first it's small—five percent toward savings, two percent toward extra debt payoff, one percent toward WPBS. It might feel almost laughable. But remember what we talked about in earlier chapters: small, consistent amounts are not small. They are seeds. They are training your mind, your habits, and your nervous system for ownership and stewardship. As your income grows and your leaks shrink, those percentages can increase.

Notice the order of operations here. In the old pattern, you paid bills, did random spending, then thought about saving and giving "if anything's left." In your new pattern, you pay essentials, you intentionally pay your future and your community, and then you enjoy what remains for joy and flexibility. That one shift—

paying the future on purpose instead of by accident—can create a completely different life over time. It turns your Money Map into a quiet machine that keeps honoring your future even on days when you're tired or tempted.

This is where WPBS fits in beautifully. When you put even a small, fixed amount each month toward your dollar-a-day commitment—about thirty dollars—you are building a habit of collective ownership. You are not waiting until you "feel rich" to participate in wealth-building. You are participating now, from where you are. Your Money Map might literally have a line that says "WPBS – Community Ownership" with a set amount. Each time you fund that line, you are reminding yourself: "I am not just paying bills. I am building something bigger than me." That awareness changes how you experience even your hardest workdays. You're not just working to survive; you're working to invest.

I want you to feel, in your body, what it is like to know where every dollar is going before it leaves. Imagine opening your banking app and seeing the same numbers, but with a different story. Instead of, "This looks okay, I guess," you see, "This part is for rent, this part is for food, this part is growing for my emergency fund, this part is heading to investments, this part is for WPBS, this part is for joy." Your money becomes less mysterious. The anxiety that used to hum in the background begins to quiet down. You are not walking through financial fog anymore. You are following a map you drew yourself.

You might worry that a Money Map will make your life feel rigid and suffocating. In reality, the opposite happens. When you decide ahead of time what your money will do, you create more freedom, not less. You are free from the stress of constantly thinking, "Can I afford this?" because you already told your money what it can and cannot do this month. You are free from the shame of overdrafts and surprises because you're looking ahead, not just looking back. You are free from the internal war between "I want to enjoy life now" and "I should be responsible" because your map makes room for both joy and responsibility.

There will be months when your Money Map goes off course. Maybe you underestimated groceries, forgot about a school event, or got hit with an unexpected repair. When that happens, resist the urge to say, "See, this doesn't work," and throw the whole plan away. Instead, treat it like a GPS recalculating. You don't abandon the map just because you took one wrong turn. You adjust. You learn. You say, "Okay, next month I'll plan for that. Next month I'll give myself a little more margin here." Over time, your Money Map becomes more accurate, and you become more confident.

I want you to notice how all of this ties back to identity. A person who sees themselves as "bad with money" will see a Money Map as a test they are destined to fail. A person who sees themselves as "learning to be a wise steward" will see a Money Map as practice. You are that second person. You are not making this map because you are perfect. You are making it because you are committed. You are saying, "I don't control everything, but I will control what I can. I may not have grown up with this skill, but I am developing it now." That attitude alone separates you from years of drifting.

Let's bring this home with a simple visualization. Close your eyes for a moment and imagine your income for next month as a group of people standing in front of you, each one representing one dollar. See yourself walking down the line, gently placing your hand on each shoulder and saying, "You—housing. You—groceries. You—transportation. You—emergency fund. You—debt payoff. You—investing. You—WPBS. You—joy." Notice how it feels to assign purpose instead of reacting later. Notice how it feels to stand there as the one in charge, calm and clear. That feeling is the essence of your Money Map. You may not have every detail worked out yet, but your spirit is practicing the posture of leadership.

As you get more comfortable with this process, you will start to see opportunities you couldn't see before. You may realize, "If I adjust this expense, I can free up more for savings." You may notice that certain "must-haves" are actually "nice-to-haves" in disguise. You may decide to downsize something for a season to accelerate your goals. Because you have a map, those decisions will feel strategic, not desperate. You'll know what you're trading and why. And when you see progress—your savings growing, your debt shrinking, your WPBS contributions stacking—you will feel encouraged to keep going.

Remember, the goal here is not to create a perfect spreadsheet. The goal is to create a conscious, intentional relationship with your money. The paper or app you use is just a tool. The real change is happening in your mind and your habits. Every time you sit down to map out your month, even if it's messy, you are reinforcing a powerful message: "I care about my future. I respect my money. I am building something." That is the mindset of an owner. That is the mindset of a WPBS Billionaire-in-Training.

As we move into the next chapters, we will talk more specifically about building your emergency cushion, using credit as a tool instead of a trap, and creating multiple streams of income. Those strategies will plug into the foundation you are building here.

Without a Money Map, those advanced moves become scattered and stressful. With a Money Map, they become part of an organized, powerful plan.

For now, I want you to carry this simple affirmation with you: "Every dollar in my life has an assignment." Say it when you get paid. Say it when you sit down to plan. Say it when you're tempted to swipe without thinking. "Every dollar in my life has an assignment." Feel how that phrase shifts you from drifting to directing. Feel how it aligns with the WPBS vision of collective intention and disciplined power.

You are no longer someone who just watches money come and go. You are someone who gives money orders. You are someone who points dollars toward destiny—for yourself, your loved ones, and your people. Your Money Map is not just ink on paper; it is a reflection of a new you emerging. And as that new you gets clearer and stronger, your financial life will begin to look more and more like the future you've been praying for.

Chapter Five

The One-Dollar Revolution: How Small Moves Build Giant Power

By now, you have seen the leaks, heard your old money stories, stepped over the line from consumer to owner, and begun to sketch your Money Map. You are starting to feel that inner shift from drifting to directing. In this chapter, I want to zoom in on one simple, almost laughably small idea: one dollar. Just one. The kind of money you might drop in a couch cushion and not bother to pick up. The kind of money you might hand to a vending machine without thinking. The kind of money that feels so small, your old mindset says, "What difference could that make?" Today, we are going to dismantle that lie. Because in the hands of a disciplined person, and especially in the hands of a disciplined people, one dollar a day is revolutionary.

There is a dangerous phrase that has robbed many people of progress: "It's just a dollar." Wrapped inside that little sentence is a whole philosophy. It says, "Small doesn't matter. Only big counts." So we wait for the big raise, the big check, the big break, the miracle amount of money that will finally make it worth changing. Until then, we shrug at the small. We treat small money like crumbs, not understanding that crumbs, gathered consistently, become bread for generations. That mentality has kept many of us standing still, waiting for the big instead of mastering the small.

I want you to hear this clearly: wealth is not built on rare, dramatic events; it is built on daily, boring, consistent moves. The magic is not in the size of one act; it is in the repetition of that act over time. One dollar a day is not about the dollar; it is about the habit, the identity, and the momentum you are building. When you commit to moving one dollar on purpose, every day, you are training your nervous system to believe, "I am the kind of person who always invests in my future and my community, no matter what." That identity is worth far more than the actual dollar.

Think about your past habits for a moment. How many times have you said, "When I have more, I'll start saving, I'll start investing, I'll start supporting movements like WPBS"? It sounds reasonable. It even sounds responsible. But it quietly delays your destiny. It pushes ownership into a fantasy future that never quite arrives. There will always be bills. There will always be reasons to wait. The truth is, if you don't learn to move small amounts when things are tight, you will not magically start moving large amounts when things are better. The muscles of discipline, giving, saving, and investing must be trained in the "little."

The One-Dollar Revolution: How Small Moves Built Giant Power

Scripture says, "He who is faithful in little will be faithful in much." Most of us shout "Amen" when we hear that, but very few of us apply it to our money on a daily level. Faithful in little might literally mean faithful with one dollar. One dollar directed. One dollar assigned. One dollar not wasted. One dollar that says, "Today, I am aligning my money with my calling." When you put that single dollar into savings, into an investment account, into your WPBS commitment, you are doing something far bigger than the number on the screen. You are flexing the faithfulness muscle.

Now picture the WPBS vision in this light. One person, one dollar a day is powerful for that person. Over a year, that becomes three hundred sixty-five dollars that did not slip through their fingers. That is three hundred sixty-five reminders that they are not just a consumer. That is three hundred sixty-five daily votes for their own future. But when a million disciplined people do the same thing, one dollar a day becomes one million dollars a day. In a month, that's roughly thirty million dollars. In a year, three hundred sixty-five million dollars. That is no longer small. That is no longer ignorable. That is the kind of capital that shapes neighborhoods, builds businesses, negotiates deals, changes the terms of how we show up in this world.

This is why I call it the One-Dollar Revolution. Not because the dollar itself is magical, but because the collective discipline is. You have seen what happens when a million people line up for a concert, a movie, a sneaker drop. Companies get rich. Shareholders smile. The culture shifts. Imagine that same collective energy pointed toward ownership. Imagine one million people quietly, steadily, without fanfare, moving one dollar every day into a shared vision of community-owned wealth. Nobody has to scream. Nobody has to beg. The numbers do the talking. The assets do the shouting. The impact does the evangelizing.

At a personal level, your one-dollar commitment is a daily conversation with your own mind. Each day, as you move that dollar, you are saying to yourself, "No matter what else happens today, I have invested in my future and my people." That means even on days when you feel behind, even on days when your boss got on your nerves, even on days when the news is depressing, you still have a small victory. Your nervous system begins to feel different. Instead of constantly feeling like life is happening to you, you get a daily moment of, "I just made something happen for us."

You might notice, as you read this, that a small argument arises in your mind. "A dollar is nothing. I need real money to change my life." That voice is familiar. It is the same voice that has talked you out of starting many things: diets, exercise routines, study plans, prayer times, new habits. It always says, "Wait until you can do it 'right.' Wait until you can go big." But you and I both know that "wait until you can go big" is usually code for "never start." I am inviting you to expose that voice and lovingly overrule it. You are not waiting for perfect. You are starting with possible.

One beautiful thing about one dollar is that you can do it even in your hardest season. You may not yet be at the point where you can move hundreds or thousands consistently; that's okay. But most days, you can find one dollar. You can find it in a canceled snack, a skipped extra, a slightly cheaper choice. You can find it in coins and small bills that used to vanish from your life without a thought. And as your situation improves, your one-dollar habit can grow into two, five, ten, thirty, a hundred. The habit is the seed. The amounts are the branches.

The One-Dollar Revolution: How Small Moves Built Giant
Power

Think of a farmer planting seeds. One seed looks like nothing. It is small, unimpressive, dry. If you judged by sight alone, you would write it off. But the farmer is not looking at the seed; the farmer is looking at the field in their imagination. They see the harvest, the crops, the abundance. They know that what looks insignificant will, when given time and care, become something that can feed families. Your one-dollar moves are seeds. WPBS is a field. Your imagination is the forecast. When you move that dollar, you are saying, "I believe in my future harvest so much, I'm willing to plant when nobody else sees it."

At the same time, the One-Dollar Revolution is about psychological safety. Large financial goals can feel intimidating and overwhelming. "Save ten thousand." "Pay off fifty thousand in debt." "Invest enough to retire." Those are important goals, but they can trigger fear and paralysis. One dollar, on the other hand, is non-threatening. It is almost playful. It allows you to begin without freaking out your nervous system. You don't have to move mountains in one day; you just have to move one dollar in the right direction. Tomorrow, you do it again. And again. And again. Before long, your brain begins to trust you. You said you would do something small and you actually did it. That builds self-respect.

If you choose, you can even turn your one-dollar move into a daily ritual. Maybe every evening, you open your banking app or physical jar and move that dollar where it belongs—into savings, an investment, or your WPBS account. As you do it, you might say a quick prayer or affirmation: "This dollar is a seed. This dollar is joining thousands of others. This dollar is building something bigger than me." Over time, that ritual becomes sacred. It is a tiny daily act of agreement with your calling.

Of course, the goal is not to only ever move one dollar. The goal is to build a lifestyle where moving money toward your future and your community is automatic. But the one-dollar commitment is like training wheels. It gets you moving. It proves to you that consistency is possible. After a few months of this, you may look up and realize, "If I can move one dollar every day without fail, maybe I can move three. Maybe I can move five. Maybe I can move my first hundred." Your sense of what's possible will expand not because someone hyped you up, but because you have a track record with yourself.

Notice how this one-dollar concept fits perfectly inside your Money Map. When you give every dollar a job, one of those jobs can be daily seed-sowing. It doesn't have to be random. It can be part of your plan. For example, your Money Map might say, "Each month, at least thirty dollars will go to WPBS." When you break that down, it is literally one dollar a day. You are not scrambling; you are following the map. That one line item, faithfully honored, is your personal connection to a massive, collective stream of capital. You are not standing on the sidelines watching other people build. You are in the flow.

On days when you are tempted to quit, I want you to remember this: revolutions are rarely loud at the beginning. They start quietly, in hearts and habits, in living rooms and late-night decisions, not just in speeches and headlines. The One-Dollar Revolution is happening every time someone like you chooses to move that "insignificant" amount with intention. It is happening every time somebody says, "Before I treat myself, I will treat my future and my people." It is happening every time we refuse to despise small beginnings.

Now, let's widen the lens again and picture what happens over years. Imagine a child growing up in a home where one-dollar discipline is normal. They watch you move that money every day or every week. They hear you explain, "This is for our future. This is how we help build our own businesses, our own properties, our own institutions." To them, giving, saving, investing, and supporting WPBS are not strange adult activities; they are just "what we do." That child grows up with ownership in their nervous system. They will not have to start from scratch like you did. That alone makes your one-dollar habit priceless.

As you sit with this idea, you might feel two things at once: a little bit of skepticism and a surprising sense of peace. The skeptical part says, "Can it really be that simple?" The peaceful part says, "I can do this." I want you to let the peaceful part win. The enemy of your progress loves to complicate things so much that you give up before you start. God, wisdom, and common sense often simplify things so that you can take the next step. One dollar a day is a simplified, next-step kind of strategy. It is not the whole plan, but it is a powerful piece of the plan.

I want you to say this with me in your mind, or even out loud if you can: "I will never again say 'It's just a dollar.' From this day forward, every dollar in my life has meaning. Every dollar is a seed. Every dollar can help build something." Feel how that declaration begins to shift the way you see loose change, small bills, and minor decisions. There is no such thing as "throwaway money" in the life of a builder. There is only money that is directed or neglected. You are choosing direction.

As we move into the next chapters—talking about emergency cushions, credit, and multiple streams of income—remember that all of those "bigger" strategies are built on the same foundation: small, consistent moves. The One-Dollar Revolution is your training ground. It is you proving, day by day, that you can show up for your future and for WPBS even when life is not perfect. And as you keep showing up, the future will begin to show up for you in ways you could not fully imagine when you started.

So tonight, or as soon as you can after reading this, I invite you to take the first step. Move one dollar on purpose. Make it visible. Make it conscious. Make it a statement. Then do it again tomorrow. And the next day. Watch what happens—not just in your account, but in your mind, your confidence, your sense of belonging to something bigger. You are not waiting for a revolution to come. You are the revolution, one dollar at a time.

Chapter Six

Credit: Lever, Not Collar

For many of us, the word "credit" comes with a whole swirl of emotions—hope, fear, shame, confusion, even a little bit of excitement. Credit can feel like that friend who helped you out when you needed them and then started acting funny when it was time to be paid back. One day it feels like a blessing, the next day it feels like a curse. In this chapter, we are going to clear the fog. We are going to stop treating credit like a mysterious, mystical force and start seeing it for what it truly is: a tool. A lever. Something you can learn to use with wisdom, instead of something that wraps around your neck like a collar.

First, let's tell the truth. Many of us were introduced to credit the wrong way. Not through education, but through desperation. Nobody sat us down at the kitchen table and said, "Here is how interest works. Here is how your credit score is calculated. Here is how lenders think. Here is how to use this to your advantage." Instead, we learned about credit when a bill was due, and the money wasn't there. When a tire blew out. When a child needed

55

something. When an emergency knocked on the door. The credit card offer came in the mail or the "buy now, pay later" button popped up on the screen, and it felt like rescue. No judgment—those decisions often came from trying to survive. But surviving and building are two different things. This chapter is about that shift.

Think of credit like a power tool. In the hands of someone trained, a power tool can build a house. In the hands of someone careless or uninformed, the same tool can cause serious damage. The tool itself is neutral. It does not love you or hate you. It does not care about your race, your neighborhood, or your feelings. It works by rules, not by emotion. When you learn the rules, you can make the tool work for you. When you ignore the rules, you end up working for the tool. That's when credit starts to feel like a collar—tightening around your neck in the form of minimum payments, high interest, and constant anxiety.

Before we go any further, I want you to release the shame. If credit has been a mess in your life, welcome to the human family. You are not the only one who has maxed out a card, missed a payment, or avoided opening a statement out of fear. You are not the only one who signed for a loan you didn't fully understand. You are not broken. You were under-taught and over-marketed to. In WPBS, we are not here to beat you up about the past. We are here to equip you for the future. Credit can be rebuilt. Credit habits can be changed. And even before the numbers change, your identity around credit can begin to heal.

I want you to imagine credit like a bridge. On one side of the bridge is where you are now. On the other side is something that costs more than you can pay for in one moment: a home, an education, a reliable car, a business expansion, an investment opportunity. Healthy credit is the bridge that allows you to cross over and access that thing in a structured, time-based way. Unhealthy credit is when you use the bridge to go on unnecessary trips—late-night emotional shopping sprees, impulse vacations, impressing people who won't remember you in six months. The bridge is the same, but where you choose to cross to makes all the difference.

Here is where the lever metaphor comes in. A lever is a simple tool that lets you move something heavy with less effort. Good credit, used wisely, can act like a lever. It can reduce the cost of borrowing through lower interest rates. It can open doors to housing, jobs, and business opportunities. It can give you space to breathe while you build. But if you throw a lever around your neck and wear it like a necklace, it becomes a weight, not a help. That's what debt feels like when it's out of control—a beautiful tool in the wrong place.

Let's talk about what credit actually measures. At its core, your credit score is a trust score. It answers one simple question: "When this person borrows, do they pay back on time?" The score doesn't measure your worth as a human being, your intelligence, your anointing, or your potential. It measures behavior over time—due dates, balances, how long you've had accounts, whether you use credit lightly or heavily. That's all. When you see it that way, the fear starts to shrink. If behavior created it, behavior can change it.

A lot of us were never taught the difference between using credit and being used by credit. Using credit means you have a plan before you borrow. You know how you will pay it back, and when, and with what money. Being used by credit means you borrow first and figure out the plan later—if at all. Using credit means keeping your balances low relative to your limits. Being used by credit means running your cards near the maximum all the time, then wondering why the score goes down and the stress goes up. Using credit means saying, "This card is a tool for convenience and protection, not an extension of my income." Being used by credit means treating the card like free money until the bill arrives and breaks the spell.

In your new life as an owner-in-training, you are going to relate to credit very differently. First, you will see it as part of your Money Map, not something separate. Your cards, loans, and payments are just another set of line items you assign and control. You decide, in advance, how much room you are willing to give to debt in your monthly plan. You don't let credit sneak up on you anymore. If you need to use a card, it's with intention: "This is for travel we planned and saved toward." "This is for a necessary expense I can pay off in full when the statement comes." If you cannot see clearly how you'll pay it off, that is a bright yellow light. Slow down and reconsider.

Here is a simple rule that can keep you out of a lot of trouble: do not finance your feelings. When we are sad, angry, lonely, or bored, credit can feel like a quick fix. "I'll buy something to feel better. I'll worry about the bill later." That is how the collar tightens. In those moments, I want you to pause and breathe. Ask yourself, "Am I buying this because I truly need it and it fits my plan, or am I trying to change how I feel?" If it's about feelings, find another way: prayer, a walk, a call to a friend, a journal, a nap, a glass of water, a chapter of this book. Your emotions deserve care, but your future doesn't deserve punishment for today's mood.

For those who are already deep in credit card debt, let's talk about the path forward. There is no magic wand, but there is a clear direction. The first step is to know the truth. List your debts: who you owe, how much you owe, interest rates, minimum payments. This part can feel painful, but remember: the pain comes from the darkness, not the light. The darkness was the avoiding, the unopened envelopes, the "I don't want to know." The light is your ally. Once the numbers are on paper, you have something to work with.

Next, you begin to prioritize. One common method is the "debt snowball"—pay minimums on everything, then put any extra toward the smallest balance. When that one is paid off, roll that payment into the next one, and so on. Another approach is the "debt avalanche"—focus extra payments on the balance with the highest interest rate, then move down the list. Both methods can work. The key is consistency. The key is deciding, "I am attacking this. I am not waiting for it to disappear on its own." Your credit becomes your project, not your enemy.

As you do this, your identity is shifting. You are no longer a person "drowning in debt." You are a person "in the process of paying off debt." You are no longer "bad with credit." You are "learning to master credit." Those small language shifts matter. They keep you from giving up when progress feels slow. They remind your subconscious that you are moving, not stuck. Yes, there will be months when life happens and you can't throw extra at the debt. That's okay. You get back to it as soon as you can. You don't quit.

Now, let's bring WPBS into this conversation, because credit doesn't just affect you as an individual; it affects our collective power. Communities with strong credit profiles can borrow at better rates, launch businesses with more ease, and negotiate from a position of strength. Communities buried in predatory debt stay on the defensive. Part of the WPBS movement is about shifting our collective relationship to credit—moving away from high-cost borrowing for consumption and toward strategic borrowing for ownership. That might look like fewer store cards for clothes and more strategic loans for purchasing properties. It might look like less emotional swiping and more planned financing for assets that produce income.

Imagine a future where thousands of WPBS participants have repaired their credit, learned to use it wisely, and then leveraged that improved standing to purchase buildings, equipment, and businesses under community-controlled entities. The cost of borrowing drops. The terms of the deals improve. Money that used to flow out of our neighborhoods in the form of high interest and late fees now stays in the ecosystem, cycling through our own institutions. That future starts with you sitting at your table, looking at your credit, and saying, "I will not let this be a collar. I will turn this into a lever."

For some, the idea of using credit at all might feel scary. Maybe you have been through a painful bankruptcy or foreclosure. Maybe you cut up every card in your wallet and swore you'd never borrow again. If that's you, honor the season you're in. Sometimes, a period of "cash only" is a necessary detox. But as you heal and grow, I want you to stay open to the possibility that you can have a different relationship with credit in the future. Not the same relationship that hurt you, but a wiser, calmer, more mature one—one where you hold the tool instead of the tool holding you.

If you are just starting out with credit or rebuilding from past damage, small, positive steps can help. A secured credit card, where you put down a deposit and use the card lightly, paid in full each month, can begin to rebuild trust. Being added as an authorized user on a trusted family member's well-managed card can sometimes help, if done carefully. Keeping utilization low—meaning you use only a small portion of whatever limit you have—sends a signal: "I am not desperate. I am disciplined." Over time, those signals add up. Your score rises not by magic, but by consistent behavior aligned with your new identity.

One important mindset shift is this: your credit score is not a grade on your soul; it is a dashboard for your strategy. If the score is low, it's data. It's telling you, "We have work to do here." If the score is improving, it's telling you, "What you're doing is working; keep going." You don't worship the number, and you don't ignore it. You respect it as feedback. As a WPBS Billionaire-in-Training, you learn to use feedback instead of being offended by it.

I also want to talk directly to the feeling of being trapped. If your debt feels overwhelming, like a weight on your chest, I want you to gently notice the story your mind is telling. Maybe it says, "I'll never get out of this. It's too much. I blew it." That story makes you feel heavy and hopeless. I invite you to try a different story: "This is a lot, but it is not impossible. Other people have walked out of worse situations. I am not alone. I am learning. I am moving. I will not stay here forever." As you read those words, allow your breath to deepen. Let your shoulders drop. The numbers on the page haven't changed yet, but the energy you're bringing to them has. That energy matters.

Credit, at its best, is boring. It's not the dramatic swipe or the shiny new card; it's the quiet rhythm of on-time payments, low balances, and wise choices. There's not much to post about. No one is clapping for you every time you decline to open a store account for an extra ten percent off. But those quiet choices are building something. They are building a reputation with lenders, a pathway to better rates, and more importantly, a reputation with yourself. You are proving that you can be trusted with agreements. That integrity spills over into other areas of your life.

As we close this chapter, I want you to picture something powerful. Imagine a collar around your neck labeled "Debt." Feel the weight of it, the restriction, the way it pulls when you try to move freely. Now imagine unlocking that collar, lifting it off, and laying it down on a workbench. On that bench, it transforms into a lever—a long, strong bar you can use to move a heavy object labeled "Asset." Home. Business. Education. Community property. You place the lever under that object, set your feet, and lean your weight into it. Slowly, with effort, the heavy thing begins to move. Same metal. Different position. Different result.

That is what you are doing as you learn to handle credit differently. You are taking something that used to choke you and turning it into something that helps you move mountains. You are not doing it overnight. You are doing it choice by choice, payment by payment, plan by plan. You are doing it as part of your larger journey—following leaks, rewriting stories, stepping into ownership, mapping your money, committing to the one-dollar revolution, and now, mastering this strange thing called credit.

Carry this affirmation with you into the days ahead: "Credit is my tool, not my master. I borrow with wisdom, I pay with integrity, and I build with purpose. My past mistakes do not define my future. I am learning, I am growing, and I am turning this lever toward my destiny and my community."

As you speak those words and act them out, credit will slowly lose its power to scare you. It will become what it was meant to be all along in your life: a neutral tool in the hands of a wise builder. And that is exactly who you are becoming.

Your Cushion of Peace: Building an Emergency Fund That Loves You Back

There is a special kind of peace that you cannot shout your way into, dance your way into, or even pray your way into without also changing your habits. It is the peace of knowing that if something breaks, you don't have to. If a bill surprises you, you don't have to fall apart. If life throws one of its infamous curveballs, you may still gasp, you may still feel it—but you don't have to go into financial panic mode. That peace has a very practical name: an emergency fund. In this chapter, we are going to stop treating an emergency fund like a luxury for "other people" and start treating it like one of the most loving gifts you can give to yourself, your future, and your participation in WPBS.

Think of an emergency fund as a cushion between you and the concrete floor of life. Without that cushion, every unexpected hit feels like a crisis. A flat tire is a crisis. A medical co-pay is a crisis. A missed shift at work is a crisis. The refrigerator dies and you feel like your whole world tilted. With a cushion, those same events might be annoying, inconvenient, even painful—but they do not have the power to knock you out. The difference is not that "bad things" stopped happening; the difference is that you gave yourself something soft to land on.

Many of us have lived for years with no cushion at all. If we're honest, we have been one paycheck, one layoff, one illness, one car problem away from chaos. That constant closeness to the edge creates a low, humming anxiety in the background of life. You might not even notice it until you try to rest. You lay down at night and your mind starts asking, "What if something happens? What if I can't work? What if they cut my hours? What if the car doesn't start?" That is not because you're weak or fearful; it is because your nervous system knows there is no backup plan. An emergency fund does not eliminate every worry, but it quiets that hum. It tells your body, "We have a little room. We are not standing on a cliff with our toes hanging over."

Let's be clear about what an emergency fund is and is not. An emergency fund is money set aside, on purpose, for real emergencies—unexpected, necessary expenses that protect your health, your ability to work, and your basic stability. It is not for sales at the mall, flash deals, "limited-time offers," or vacations you didn't plan for. It is not a "fun fund." It is a seriousness fund. It is a "keep the lights on when life flips the switch" fund. When you treat it that way, it becomes sacred.

Right now, your old story might be trying to interrupt. "I can't even keep up with my bills. How am I supposed to save for emergencies?" That's a fair question. But I want you to consider this: you are already paying for emergencies—just in a more expensive, stressful way. Without a cushion, you pay with overdraft fees, late fees, high-interest credit card balances, payday loans, borrowing from friends and family, and the mental cost of constant worry. An emergency fund does not add a new burden; it slowly replaces those heavier burdens with a lighter, quieter one. It is like choosing to carry a backpack instead of dragging a boulder.

Imagine future you, a year or two from now, with a small but real emergency fund sitting quietly in a savings account. The car makes a strange noise. Instead of your heart dropping into your stomach, you take a breath and say, "Okay. Let's check the fund." You still don't like spending the money; nobody enjoys that. But you do it from a place of strength instead of desperation. Then, over the next months, you refill the cushion, like fluffing a pillow that got a little compressed. That rhythm—use, refill, protect— creates resilience.

Start by giving yourself permission to build this cushion slowly. You do not need a perfect number before you can feel safer. Many financial experts talk about having three to six months of expenses saved. That is a beautiful goal. But if that number feels so huge that your brain wants to shut down, let's start smaller. Your first milestone might be just one hundred dollars set aside. Then two hundred fifty. Then five hundred. Then one thousand. Each level you reach changes something in you. A hundred dollars says, "I am no longer completely exposed." Five hundred says, "I can handle some basic emergencies." A thousand says, "Life can hit, and I can breathe."

This is where your Money Map and your One-Dollar Revolution work together. You already decided to give every dollar a job. One of those jobs is "emergency fund builder." Maybe it's ten dollars a week. Maybe it's twenty-five. Maybe it's the spare change you sweep automatically into a savings account. Maybe it's that one extra shift you take once a month, dedicated entirely to your cushion. You are not waiting for leftover money to wander into savings by accident. You are sending it there on purpose, even if it's a small amount.

As you do this, your identity shifts again. You are no longer the person who says, "I can't save." Instead, you say, "I am building my cushion of peace." You are no longer the person who says, "Something always comes up and ruins my plan." Instead, you say, "When something comes up, I am more ready each time." Notice how that sounds in your own ears. Feel how different it is to speak about emergencies from a place of growing readiness rather than helplessness.

I want you to visualize your emergency fund as an actual cushion sitting on a chair with your name on it. Right now, that cushion might be thin. It might even look like just a folded towel. That's okay. You walk over to it with a small piece of stuffing in your hand—today's five dollars, today's ten dollars—and you tuck it inside. The cushion plumps up, just a little. Tomorrow, you do it again. Next week, again. Month after month, the cushion gets thicker. You don't brag about it. You don't post selfies with it. But you know it's there. And every time you walk past that chair in your mind, you stand a little taller.

There will be times when you are tempted to use your emergency fund for non-emergencies. A trip you really want to take. A sale that feels too good to pass up. A moment when your emotions say, "We deserve this, and the money is right there." In those moments, I want you to pause and talk to yourself like a wise parent. "Yes, we do deserve joy. Yes, we do deserve good things.

Your Cusion of Peace: Building an Emergency Fund That Loves You Back

But we also deserve safety. We deserve to not panic every time life happens. Let's protect the cushion and find another way." You are not punishing yourself; you are protecting yourself.

Now, let's connect this to WPBS. Some people might say, "Should I build an emergency fund first and then participate in WPBS?" That's like asking, "Should I breathe in first or breathe out?" You need both. Your emergency fund protects your personal stability; WPBS participation connects you to community-level stability and power. One is a personal oxygen mask; the other is building an oxygen system for the whole cabin. You may adjust the amounts at different stages of your journey, but both belong in the picture. You can say, "I am building my cushion and I am contributing to our collective cushion."

Imagine a community where thousands of people have at least a small emergency fund. When job losses happen, when crises hit, when unexpected bills show up, fewer families are thrown into total freefall. There is still strain, but there is a bit more time to think, plan, and respond. Now add WPBS to that picture—community-owned businesses and resources that can provide jobs, discounts, and support in those hard times. Your personal cushion plus our shared cushion creates layers of protection. That is the difference between a community that is constantly in survival mode and a community that can breathe, strategize, and build.

You might be thinking, "Every time I try to save, something happens and I have to spend it. What's the point?" Here is the point: if you had not saved, that "something" would have hit you even harder. The fund did exactly what it was supposed to do. It absorbed the blow. Yes, you may have to rebuild it. Yes, it can feel discouraging to see the balance go down. But instead of saying,

"I can never get ahead," I want you to practice saying, "Thank God I had it. I'm grateful I could handle this. Now we refill the cushion." That gratitude keeps you from resenting the very tool that is saving you.

Sometimes, building an emergency fund will require short-term sacrifice. You may choose to cut back on certain pleasures for a season. You might decide, "For the next six months, I am going to lower my entertainment spending to build my cushion faster." Instead of seeing that as punishment, see it as a training camp. Athletes train differently before a big game. Soldiers prepare differently before a mission. You are doing the same with your money. There will be a time to upgrade and enjoy more. Right now, you are laying a foundation.

In practical terms, keep your emergency fund somewhere you can access when needed, but not so easily that you constantly dip into it for non-emergencies. A basic savings account linked to your checking can work. You don't need to chase high returns here; the primary purpose is safety and availability, not maximum growth. Think of it as financial body armor, not a race car. You want it dependable, not flashy.

As your cushion grows, something beautiful begins to happen in your decision-making. You stop making choices out of panic. You become less vulnerable to predatory lenders and quick-fix offers. You can say no to unfair terms because you are not negotiating from empty pockets. You can leave toxic jobs or living situations more safely because you have a little runway. That runway might not be luxurious, but it is real. It gives you options. Options are a form of power.

Your children, grandchildren, or younger people in your life will notice this, even if you never give a formal lecture. They will see you responding to crises differently. They will see you say, "We had an unexpected expense, but we're okay. We have a fund for that." That sentence alone can change how they feel about money. They learn that life can be hard and stable at the same time. They learn that planning is a form of love. They learn that being prepared is not paranoia; it is wisdom.

If shame or regret tries to creep in while you read this—regret that you didn't start sooner, shame that you're starting with so little—I want you to gently push back. "I am starting now. That is what matters. Today is the day I begin to build my cushion of peace." You can't go back and save for yesterday's emergencies. But you can decide that next year's emergencies will meet a stronger, wiser, better-prepared version of you.

Take a moment and imagine yourself one year from now with a modest but real emergency fund—whatever that number is for you. See yourself logging into your account, looking at that cushion, and feeling a wave of calm. Hear yourself saying, "We're not where we want to be yet, but look how far we've come. Last year, we had nothing. Now we have this. And we're still building." Let that image settle into your nervous system. That is not fantasy; that is a future you can help create with each small deposit.

Now imagine five years from now. You have weathered some storms. The car broke down once or twice. Someone got sick. The water heater died. Life happened. Each time, you drew on your fund, then refilled it. Over time, your cushion grew thicker, not thinner. You also invested. You participated in WPBS. You built. When new opportunities arise—job changes, business chances, property possibilities—you are not scrambling in panic. You are weighing options from a place of relative stability. That version of you is not luckier than you. They are simply the result of you deciding, here and now, to prioritize peace.

As we prepare to move into the next chapters, where we will talk about creating multiple streams of income and teaching the next generation, remember this: your emergency fund is not a side project; it is central. It gives your other money moves room to breathe. It allows you to invest without constantly raiding your investments whenever life hiccups. It allows you to support WPBS without feeling like one unexpected bill will knock you out of the movement. It keeps you in the game.

Carry this affirmation with you: "I am building my cushion of peace. Every small deposit is a declaration that I will not live on the edge forever. I honor my future by protecting my present." Say it when you move five dollars. Say it when you move fifty. Say it when you move that first hundred. Each time, feel the ground under your feet get just a little more solid.

You are not just saving money; you are buying back your peace, one deposit at a time. You are not just protecting yourself; you are modeling stability for everyone who watches you. And you are not just preparing for emergencies; you are creating the calm, confident foundation from which you can help build a new future—for yourself, for your family, and for the WPBS community you are a vital part of.

Many Rivers, One Ocean: Creating Multiple Streams of Income

Up to now, we've been doing some powerful internal work. You've followed the leaks. You've rewritten your money stories. You've stepped from consumer toward owner. You've given every dollar a job. You've joined the One-Dollar Revolution. You've started to tame credit and build your cushion of peace. That alone is life-changing. But at some point on this journey, a new question rises up from deep inside you: "What if more money could flow toward me in honorable, sustainable ways?" Not from the lottery, not from wishful thinking, but from the gifts, skills, and grit God already placed in you. This chapter is about that shift—from one paycheck, one stream, one fragile source—to multiple streams, like rivers feeding an ocean.

For a long time, many of us were trained to think in terms of one job, one income, one paycheck. You go to work, you get paid every week or every other week, you pay your bills, and you repeat. If that one source is healthy, you feel okay. If that one source is threatened—layoffs, cut hours, changes in leadership—your entire life feels shaky. That is a lot of pressure to place on one stream. Imagine an entire city getting all its water from one pipe. Any disruption becomes a crisis. Multiple streams are not about greed; they are about stability and options.

Picture your financial life as a landscape. Right now, you may have one river running through it—your primary job or business. It flows. Some months heavier, some months lighter. What we want to do is look for other potential streams, creeks, and channels that can begin to trickle in and eventually flow. They don't all have to be massive. Some might be small side incomes. Some might be seasonal. Some might be long-term investments that start tiny and grow over time. The point is not to overwhelm yourself but to recognize that you are allowed to have more than one way money comes into your life.

There is a story many of us inherited that says, "Be grateful you have a job. Don't ask for more. Don't rock the boat. Don't dream too big." Gratitude is good. But gratitude without growth turns into stagnation. You can be deeply grateful for what you have and still believe there is more inside you. You can say, "Thank you, Lord, for this job," and also say, "And thank You for the ideas, the creativity, the talents, and the relationships that can open additional doors." Multiple streams of income are not about chasing money; they are about fully honoring what God put in you by allowing it to produce in different ways.

Many Rivers, One Ocean: Creating Multiple Streams of Income

I want you to pause and think about your gifts. Not your job title. Not your resume. Your gifts. Are you a good listener? A problem solver? A teacher? A storyteller? Are you great with children, elders, technology, organizing chaos, making people laugh, fixing things, cooking, encouraging others, designing, writing, planning? Those gifts are not random. They are clues. They are hints about where additional streams might flow. Sometimes we are so used to our own abilities that we underestimate them. We say, "Oh, that's just something I do." But for someone else, what you do "naturally" is exactly what they need and are willing to pay for.

Multiple streams start when you stop saying, "I'm just a…" and start saying, "I also am a…" "I also am a tutor." "I also am a coach." "I also am a consultant." "I also bake." "I also design." "I also fix." "I also write." One job may still be your main river for now, but you begin to see that your identity is bigger than your job description. Once that inner shift happens, your brain starts asking new questions: "How could this gift serve others in a way that brings in income?" "How could this skill become a service?" Those questions are fertile soil.

Let's be very clear about something: not every talent has to become a hustle. You are not required to monetize every joy. Some things are meant to be hobbies, pure and simple. But some talents are indeed assignments. They are meant to feed you and others. The key is discernment. Ask yourself, "Does this activity drain me or energize me? Do I feel a sense of calling when I do this? Are people already asking me for help in this area?" If the answer is yes, there may be a stream there. Start small, prayerfully, and with a plan.

In the context of WPBS, multiple streams take on an even deeper meaning. You are not just trying to "get the bag" for yourself. You are building the capacity to invest, to participate, to show up as more than a consumer. When you have more income streams, you have more flexibility to support your dollar-a-day commitment, to invest in community-owned projects, to buy from Black-owned businesses, to help family without sinking yourself, to sow into ministries and missions that matter to you. More streams equal more ways to say yes to your assignment.

You might say, "I'm already tired with one job. How am I supposed to add more?" That is a real concern, and it's why we have to be wise. Multiple streams should not mean multiple breakdowns. We are not glorifying burnout. Instead, we are looking for smart, sustainable, and sometimes slow-growing ways to diversify your income. That might mean a stream that only flows on weekends. It might mean a stream that is mostly passive after an initial setup—like a digital product, rental income, or small investments. It might mean rearranging your time so that you cut some low-value activities to make room for a stream that can bless you and others.

Think of a season in your life where you were already giving time away for free. Maybe you were always helping people with resumes, always advising folks about their business ideas, always babysitting, always baking, always doing hair, always troubleshooting their phone or computer. For a season, you may choose to keep some of that as pure ministry. But you are also allowed to say, "This is a skill. This is a service. I can structure this as a side business or extra stream." You move from "random favors" to "organized service," with clear boundaries, fair pricing, and an understanding that your time has value.

Many Rivers, One Ocean: Creating Multiple Streams of Income

Some streams might come through education and training. Maybe there is a certification that could boost your value in the marketplace. Maybe there is a skill—coding, project management, bookkeeping, graphic design, counseling—that you could sharpen to open doors for contract work, remote work, or consulting. When you see yourself as a builder, you don't just show up to your job and go home. You also ask, "What skills can I add over the next one to three years that will give me more options?" That question alone can change your trajectory.

Multiple streams also protect your mental health. When everything in your life is tied to one job or one income source, the emotional pressure is intense. You may tolerate situations that harm you because you feel you have no choice. When you begin to build other streams, even small ones, your posture changes. You may stay at that job for a while, but you know, in the back of your mind, "I am not completely trapped. I have something else brewing. I have other ways value flows through me." That awareness alone can help you make clearer decisions.

Now, let's talk about timing. You don't have to launch three side businesses next week. In fact, please don't. Instead, choose one stream to explore first. Ask, "What is the easiest, most natural way for me to begin bringing in a little extra income within the next sixty to ninety days?" It might be selling a product or service to people you already know. It might be offering your skills on a freelance platform. It might be picking up a part-time gig that aligns with your strengths and doesn't deplete your soul. Start there. Let that stream teach you.

Your Money Map will help you aim those new dollars. You can decide in advance, "This extra income stream is for debt payoff," or "This one is for emergency fund building," or "This one is for

WPBS and long-term investments." When you give a new stream a specific mission, you can see its impact more clearly. That clarity keeps you motivated on days when you are tired and tempted to quit. Instead of thinking, "This little extra isn't worth it," you think, "This extra is shaving months off my debt timeline," or "This extra is helping me reach my cushion goal faster," or "This extra is funding our piece of the next community asset."

As you imagine new streams, guard your heart against comparison. It's easy to look online and see people claiming to make huge sums from side hustles, trading, or trendy businesses. Many of those stories are exaggerated, incomplete, or simply not aligned with your life. Your streams do not have to impress social media. They have to serve your real life. They have to match your values, your energy, your responsibilities, and your season. A quiet, steady extra four hundred dollars a month that you actually maintain is better than a flashy idea that burns you out in three weeks.

I also want you to remember rest. Multiple streams without rest turns you into a slave to your own ambition. That is not what we are building. We are building a life where you have more options and more alignment, not more chains. Your body is not a machine. You are allowed to have days where you don't hustle, don't produce, don't answer, don't sell. In fact, you need them. Think like a farmer: there are planting seasons, growing seasons, harvesting seasons, and resting seasons. You cannot harvest year-round without destroying the soil. Your mind and body are the soil of your streams. Protect them.

In the WPBS vision, multiple streams extend beyond individual efforts. As our collective capital grows, we can create streams that employ others. A community-owned grocery store is a stream for the people who work there. A clinic is a stream for the medical professionals and staff. A construction company is a stream for the tradespeople. A community-owned tech hub is a stream for innovators and coders. Your personal streams and the community's streams feed each other. You bring your increased capacity into WPBS; WPBS creates more opportunities for you and others to earn, build, and own. That is the virtuous cycle we are aiming for.

You might not yet see exactly what your streams will look like. That's okay. This chapter is about getting your mind ready. I want you to begin asking new questions in your daily life. When you solve a problem at work, ask, "Is this a skill people pay for?" When someone compliments you on something you did—planning an event, decorating, teaching, fixing—ask yourself, "Is there a way to package this as a service?" When you notice a need in your community, ask, "Could that need be met through a small business, a side gig, or a community-owned project?" You are training your brain to see streams where before you saw only struggles.

There is also a spiritual dimension here. When you activate more of your gifts, you are not just increasing income; you are increasing impact. You will meet new people. You will step into circles you would not have entered otherwise. You will have conversations, connections, and opportunities to shine your light. Your streams become channels through which your calling flows. In that sense, multiple streams are not just about money; they are about ministry and mission.

Now, take a moment and imagine a future version of you, maybe three to five years from now, with three or four streams of income. Perhaps you have your main job or business, a side service you offer, some investments working quietly in the background, and participation in WPBS and other community ventures. Your Money Map reflects all of these. When one stream has a slow month, the others keep flowing. You are not invincible, but you are more resilient. You have more choices. You feel less desperate and more deliberate. That version of you is not a fantasy. They are built from choices you make in the next twelve months.

As we move into the later chapters, where we will talk about teaching the next generation and building a lasting legacy, remember this metaphor: many rivers, one ocean. Your paycheck is one river. Your side hustle is another. Your investments are another. WPBS is another. Together, they flow into the ocean of your life's work, your family's stability, and your community's transformation. No single river has to do everything. They work together.

Carry this affirmation with you: "I am open to multiple honest, healthy streams of income. My gifts, skills, and experiences are allowed to bless me and others. I do not chase money; I create value, and I let money flow toward that value." Say it when ideas come. Say it when fear says, "Who do you think you are?" Say it when you're tempted to shrink back into "I'm just…"

You are not "just" anything. You are a builder with many tools. You are a river-maker. You are a WPBS Billionaire-in-Training, learning to let many streams flow from the one Source. And as those streams increase, so will your ability to live, give, and build in ways that honor the God who gave you the vision and the community that needs you fully awakened.

Chapter Nine

Family Wealth Codes: Teaching the Next Generation While You're Still Learning

There is a quiet moment that happens in almost every family. A child, a grandchild, a niece, a nephew, looks up at an adult and asks, "Are we rich?" Or, "Why can't we get that?" Or, "How come some people have big houses and we don't?" In that moment, you are not just answering a curious question—you are writing code into their mind. You are shaping how they will think about money, wealth, and possibility for years to come. This chapter is about those moments. It is about the words, habits, and stories that become your family wealth codes—the unspoken programming that either passes down struggle or passes down strength. And here is the good news: you do not have to have it all figured out before you start teaching. You can teach while you're still learning.

Many of us did not grow up with healthy family wealth codes. We grew up with survival codes. "Don't ask for nothing when we go in this store." "Money doesn't grow on trees." "We don't have it." "What do you think, I'm made of money?" "As long as the lights are on, we're fine." Those phrases were not meant to hurt us; they were shields. They were the best our caregivers knew how to do with the pressure they were under. But those words also carried messages: we are always on the edge, money is mysterious and scarce, wanting more is dangerous or selfish. If we don't rewrite those messages, we will pass the same stress, fear, and limitations forward—wrapped in different clothes, but with the same core.

Imagine for a moment that your family is a computer system and your words are lines of code. Every time you say, "We're always broke," you are typing that into the operating system of the next generation. Every time you say, "We'll never get ahead," you are installing that program. But every time you say, "We are learning," "We are building," "We are owners in training," you are installing a different program. You may still be working through your own bugs and glitches, but the code you choose now determines whether your children start where you started… or start further ahead.

I want to relieve some pressure off you right now: you do not have to be "rich" to teach rich thinking. You do not need a perfect credit score, a fully funded retirement, or a house paid in full to begin imparting wisdom. In fact, some of the most powerful lessons you can teach will come from your own journey out of confusion and into clarity. You can look a young person in the eyes and say, "I didn't know these things when I was your age. I made mistakes. I learned the hard way. I still don't have it all together. But we are not going to let ignorance be our family tradition. We are learning this together." That humility and honesty carries more weight than pretending to be perfect.

Let's talk about how we speak in front of children. Kids are always listening—even when you think they're glued to a screen. They hear you talking about bills, debt, work, and money. They feel the tension in your voice when you say, "Lord, how am I going to pay this?" or when the phone rings and you let it go to voicemail because you suspect it's a collector. They might not know the details, but they feel the energy. They are learning, from the atmosphere, whether money is a constant threat or a manageable challenge. They are learning whether we run money or money runs us.

From this chapter forward, I want you to imagine that everything you say about money in front of children is being recorded and played back in their heads on repeat. That doesn't mean you lie or pretend. It means you choose your words with intention. Instead of, "We're broke," you might say, "Money is tight right now, but we're making a plan." Instead of, "We can't afford that," you might say, "That's not in our plan right now, but let's talk about how we could work toward something like that in the future." Instead of, "People like us never have anything," you might say, "People like us are learning to build and own more and more." Do you feel the difference? One set of phrases locks doors. The other set cracks them open.

Family wealth codes are not just spoken, they are acted. Children learn from what you do more than what you say. When they see you follow your Money Map, even in small ways, they are learning structure. When they see you move your one dollar a day toward WPBS or into savings, they are learning consistency. When they see you say "no" to something you want now so you can say "yes" to something bigger later, they are learning delayed gratification. They may roll their eyes. They may say, "You're doing too much." But your example is going into their internal library. One day, when life squeezes them, they will reach for those books.

You can make this teaching intentional with simple family rituals. Maybe once a week, you have a ten-minute "money huddle" at the table. You don't dump adult stress on kids, but you invite them into age-appropriate conversations. You might say, "This week, here's what we're doing with our money: paying bills, adding a little to the emergency fund, putting something toward WPBS, and enjoying a treat." You can ask, "Does anyone have a money question?" You can talk about needs versus wants. You can celebrate small wins: "We paid off a bill. We reached our first hundred dollars in savings. We kept our commitment to the one-dollar revolution this month." The goal is not to turn children into accountants; the goal is to make wise money stewardship feel normal.

Teaching the next generation while you're still learning also looks like inviting them into your growth, not hiding it. You might say to a teenager, "I used to swipe cards without thinking. Now I'm learning how interest works and how to use credit wisely. Let me show you what I've learned." Or, "I didn't know about emergency funds growing up. We're building one now. Here's why it matters." You are not lecturing from a mountaintop; you are walking with them up the hill. That shared journey builds trust. It also gives them permission to be learners, not just performers.

Let's talk about allowances and earnings. If you give a child money, you are not just giving them spending power; you are giving them a chance to practice. Instead of only teaching kids how to spend, teach them how to divide. You might introduce a simple 3-part system: give, save, spend. A portion goes to giving—church, charity, or a cause like WPBS. A portion goes to saving—for something they want or for a future cushion. A portion goes to spending—so they can experience enjoyment and choice. When a child learns to do this with ten dollars, they are rehearsing the same principles they will need with a thousand, ten thousand, and beyond.

You can take this further by tying money to contribution. Instead of only giving an automatic allowance, you might design ways they can earn more by serving—taking on extra responsibilities, helping with family projects, using their skills. This is not about turning your home into a sweatshop; it's about linking money to value. When young people understand that money is an echo of the value they bring, not a random gift from the universe, they approach work and opportunity differently. They stop seeing money as magic and start seeing it as a result.

There is another layer of family wealth codes that often goes unspoken: how we talk about "rich people." If children constantly hear, "Rich people are greedy," "Rich folks don't care about us," "If you get money, you'll change," they may unconsciously fear their own success. They might self-sabotage to stay "good" in your eyes. Do some wealthy people behave badly? Absolutely. But money simply amplifies what is already in the heart. In WPBS, we are not trying to raise selfish millionaires; we are raising generous, wise, community-minded people who can handle resources. So instead of painting all wealth with a negative brush, we can say, "Some people misuse money. But in our family, if God blesses us with more, we will use it well—to help, to build, to bless."

Passing down wealth codes also means passing down information. Too many families have had to scramble after a loved one passed because no one knew where accounts were, whether there was insurance, who was on the deed, or what the wishes were. That chaos is a form of generational theft. It robs survivors of peace, and sometimes of assets they never knew existed. Part of teaching while you're still learning is getting your own documents in order. A simple will. Clear beneficiaries on accounts. Basic life insurance if possible. A list of important information stored safely. You don't have to be morbid. You can frame it as love: "I'm putting things in place so that when my time comes, you're not left confused." That is also financial literacy. That is also WPBS.

You might feel resistance rise up at this point. "Who am I to talk about wealth when I'm still paying off debt?" "How can I teach when I'm behind?" That resistance is understandable, but I want you to consider this: precisely because you are in process, you are qualified. You know what confusion feels like. You know what poor decisions cost. You know what it feels like to say, "Never again." The next generation doesn't need your perfection; they need your authenticity. They need to see someone refuse to give up, someone willing to say, "I didn't know this before, but I'm learning now, and I refuse to let this knowledge die with me."

WPBS adds a powerful collective dimension to these family codes. When your child hears you talk about "our" businesses, "our" properties, "our" bank, "our" clinic, "our" community investments, something clicks. They begin to see wealth not only as individual success but as shared power. They understand that their participation and discipline are not just for their own house but for the larger house—the neighborhood, the Diaspora, the people. That understanding can keep them grounded. It can protect them from the illusion that "making it out" means abandoning where they came from. Instead, they can learn that real success means building bridges back.

Imagine family gatherings a few years from now. Instead of only talking about gossip, old drama, and who cooked what, there are moments where someone says, "How's your emergency fund going?" "Who started a new stream this year?" "What's the latest with WPBS?" "Who updated their will?" "Who paid off a card?" These conversations don't have to dominate the day. They can be short, celebratory, and encouraging. But their presence sends a signal: in this family, money is not a taboo or a terror. It is a topic we can discuss with honesty and hope.

For younger children, stories and games can carry wealth codes in gentle ways. You might make up stories about a character who learns to save before spending everything. You might play "store" or "bank" with play money, teaching them to count, make choices, and understand that when the money is gone, it's gone. You might create little challenges: "If you can save this amount by this date, I'll match a portion." These are simple, but they plant seeds of discipline, patience, and creativity.

For older kids and teens, you can involve them in bigger discussions. Show them how much things cost—not to scare them, but to inform them. Let them see a utility bill, a grocery receipt, the cost of a car repair. Ask, "If you were in charge of this, how would you handle it?" Let them help plan a family outing within a budget. Let them see you saying no to something cool because it does not fit the plan—and talk about why. When they ask for something expensive, don't just say yes or no; make it a conversation about value, timing, and trade-offs.

As you do all this, keep your tone rooted in love, not fear. Fear says, "You better not mess up like I did." Love says, "I want you to have it better than I did, and I'm going to share what I've learned." Fear says, "We can't." Love says, "We're learning how." Fear says, "Don't ask questions." Love says, "Ask me anything; if I don't know, we'll find out together." Your tone will echo louder than your exact words.

I want you to picture, just for a moment, a future scene. A grown child or grandchild of yours is sitting with their own child, explaining how money works. They say, "My mom, my dad, my granddad, my grandma, they didn't grow up with all this knowledge. They had to figure it out. I remember them sitting at the table, learning, budgeting, talking about WPBS, fixing their credit, building a cushion. They taught me as they learned. They didn't hide it. Because of them, I started earlier. I made fewer mistakes. And now I'm teaching you." Hear that? That is generational wealth talking. Not just in dollars, but in wisdom.

Family wealth codes also include how we respond to failure. When a child makes a money mistake—loses some cash, spends foolishly, breaks something—there is a teaching moment. The old code might say, "See, this is why you can't have nothing," shaming them and confirming a negative identity. The new code says, "This was a mistake. Let's talk about what happened, how it felt, and what we can do differently next time. You're not 'bad with money.' You're learning. This is part of learning." That distinction can be the difference between a young person shutting down and a young person growing up.

As we near the end of this chapter, I want you to feel something deep in your spirit: you are not just fixing your own finances; you are reprogramming a bloodline. You are interrupting patterns that may have been in motion for generations. You are installing new defaults: saving instead of only spending, investing instead of only consuming, planning instead of only reacting, community-building instead of only individual scrambling. The children watching you now may not fully understand it yet, but their children will live inside the world you are shaping.

Take a moment and place your hand over your heart. Whisper to yourself, "I am a carrier of new codes." Feel the weight of that, not as a burden, but as an honor. God trusted you to live at this moment, with this knowledge, with this possibility. WPBS is not just a book or a program; it is part of a new set of instructions being written into families in West Philadelphia and across the African Diaspora. Instructions that say, "We are worthy of owning. We are capable of planning. We are committed to learning. We are building something our ancestors prayed for and our descendants will thank us for."

As we move into the next chapter, where we will talk more about legacy and long-term planning, hold onto this truth: you do not have to be finished to be fruitful. You can teach while you're still learning. You can model while you're still maturing. You can bless the next generation even as you are healing from what the last generation didn't know.

Carry this affirmation with you: "In my family, the struggle stops and the building begins with me. I speak life, wisdom, and hope about money. I share what I learn. I refuse to pass down fear. I am writing new wealth codes for my bloodline."

Say it when you feel behind. Say it when you explain a bill. Say it when you move your one-dollar seed. Say it when your child asks, "Are we rich?" You might smile and answer, "We are getting richer in wisdom every day. And with that wisdom, we are learning to build the kind of wealth that blesses our family and our community for generations to come."

88

Chapter Ten

More Than Obituaries and Bills: Building a Legacy That Outlives You

One day, people you love will be standing in a room, saying your name in the past tense. That's not morbid; that's reality. They might be in a church, a funeral home, a living room, or a small office with a stack of papers in front of them. There will be tears, stories, laughter, maybe even a few secrets revealed. In that moment, you will not be there to explain yourself, fix anything, or answer questions. But your decisions will be in the room. Your planning will be in the room. Your legacy will be in the room. And I want you to hear this clearly: your legacy is more than your obituary and your clothes. It is more than who gets the TV and who gets the car. In this chapter, we are going to talk about building a legacy that outlives you—so that when your name is spoken in the past tense, your work is still speaking in the present.

For many of us, money talks have been about "right now." Can we pay this? Can we fix that? Can we make it to Friday? The idea of planning for what happens when we die sounds far away, heavy, or even disrespectful—like we're calling something on ourselves. So we avoid it. We say, "I'll get to it," and then we don't. Meanwhile, the clock is moving. Time is doing what time does. The truth is, planning for after you're gone is not about being negative; it's about being loving. It's about saying, "I care about you enough not to leave you confused, empty-handed, and fighting over nonsense when I'm no longer here."

I want you to imagine two families. In the first family, Big Mama passes away with no will, no clear instructions, and no life insurance. Nobody knows exactly what she owned or owed. There's a house with her name on the deed, but no one is sure who she meant to have it. Some folks want to sell. Some want to stay. Old arguments wake up from the dead. People are grieving, but they're also stressed, angry, and scattered. The second family loses their matriarch too—but she left a simple will, a basic policy, clear beneficiaries, and a letter explaining her wishes. People still grieve. They still cry. But there is order. There is direction. There is less confusion. Which family do you want yours to be?

Legacy is not just what you leave; it's what you set in motion. It's the way your life continues to bless people who never met you. It's the reason a child you'll never see in person will still be living under a roof you helped secure, going to a school your choices funded, working in a business your community owns. Legacy is when your decisions keep preaching long after your voice has gone quiet. And let's be clear: you are building a legacy whether you plan it or not. Dying without a plan is a kind of legacy too—it just happens to be the kind that costs your people extra money, extra pain, and sometimes the very assets you worked for.

Right now, I want you to release the idea that legacy is only for rich people. That is a lie poverty tells to keep you from preparing. Wealthy families have attorneys and big portfolios, yes. But legacy at its core is about intention. It's about saying, "This is who I want to bless, this is how I want to bless them, and this is how I want my story to continue." You can have a modest income and still have a powerful legacy if you are deliberate. A small life insurance policy, a paid-off car, a little house, a savings account with clear beneficiaries, a share in WPBS—these are seeds of legacy when handled with purpose.

Let's talk about one of the most avoided tools: a will. A will is simply a written, legal document that says, "When I leave this earth, here is where I want my things, my responsibilities, and my blessings to go." That's it. It's not a curse. It's not an invitation for death to come faster. It's a love letter combined with a game plan. Without a will, the state where you live will decide who gets what, based on default rules that do not know your family dynamics, your blended relationships, your estranged cousin, your Godchild you love like your own. The law does not know your heart. A will lets your heart speak.

You do not have to be a lawyer to understand the power of this. Imagine your loved ones, already grieving, now being told, "We don't know who owns what. This will have to go through the courts. It may take months, even years." Bills keep coming. Property taxes don't care who is still crying. If no one keeps up, properties can be lost. One of the saddest phrases in our community is, "We lost the family house." Sometimes that loss came not from an enemy, but from a lack of paperwork.

Legacy-building says, "Not on my watch." It says, "If I leave a house, I'm also leaving clarity about that house. If I leave a car, the title will not be a mystery. If I have accounts, someone will know where they are and what to do." You don't have to create a 50-page legal document. Even a simple, legally valid will and a clear list of assets and wishes can shift your family's future. This is part of being a WPBS Billionaire-in-Training: you don't just think about how to get assets—you think about how to keep them in the family and in the community on purpose.

Now let's talk about a subject many avoid until it's too late: life insurance. Some of us have seen more "GoFundMe funerals" than we can count. Families are devastated, not only emotionally, but financially. Everybody is scrambling—pulling from rent, maxing out cards, passing the plate, doing fish fries, selling plates, begging strangers online, just to bury someone. That is not a judgment; it is a reality. And it is a reality we do not have to accept as normal forever.

Life insurance is not about "getting paid" when someone dies. It is about protection, dignity, and continuity. A basic policy can mean the difference between your family inheriting a crisis and inheriting a cushion. It can mean funeral costs are covered without debt. It can mean there is money to catch up on bills, keep the house from going into foreclosure, help children adjust while the family finds its new footing. In larger amounts, it can be used to pay off mortgages, seed college funds, or even contribute to community investments that carry your name.

If you have been avoiding life insurance because it feels scary, I want you to flip the script. It is not a bet against your life; it is a vote for your family's stability. You can say, "I pray to live a long, healthy life. But whenever my time comes, early or late, my people will not be left out here scrambling." That is love with paperwork. That is affection with policy numbers. That is legacy.

Some of you might be thinking, "But I don't even know where to start. This sounds complicated." That's your old story trying to keep you stuck. Remember what we've been doing this whole book—breaking big things down into small, doable moves. Legacy planning is no different. You don't have to tackle everything in one day. You can start with a simple list:

Who do I want to bless?

What do I have right now—no matter how small—that I could pass on?

What do I want to happen to my things, my responsibilities, and my digital life (passwords, accounts) when I'm gone?

Writing these answers down is your first step. From there, you can reach out for help—whether that's a lawyer, a trusted advisor, or reputable tools and templates. You're not alone in this. You're just making the decision to begin.

I want you to think about another dimension of legacy: values and instructions. Money without wisdom can evaporate in a single generation. We've all seen it—someone receives a payout, a house, or an inheritance, and within a few years, it's gone. Not because they are evil, but because no one ever taught them what to do with it. So part of your legacy plan is not just dollars and deeds; it's guidance.

You can write a simple "Legacy Letter" to your family. In it, you can say things like: "Here's what I want you to know about how I see money. Here's why I participated in WPBS. Here's what I hope you'll do with what I leave. Here's what I learned the hard way. Here's what I want you to avoid. Here's how I hope you'll treat each other." That letter becomes a spiritual and emotional GPS that travels with the money. It won't control people's choices, but it will give them a north star when their grief and their options collide.

Now, let's link this back to WPBS on a bigger scale. Legacy is not only about your individual family. It's also about your people. WPBS is a vehicle for community legacy. When you contribute your dollar a day, when you support your local chapter, when you help own a piece of a business or property through WPBS structures, you are creating assets that do not die when you do. You are participating in something designed to outlive all of us.

Imagine this: decades from now, a young person walks into a community bank, a clinic, a co-op grocery store, or a tech hub with the WPBS name on the door. They are there to work, bank, get care, build a company, or attend a training. On the wall, there is a plaque with names—people who believed, contributed, and stayed consistent, even when it was only "one dollar" at a time. Your name is there. Maybe their parent or grandparent points and says, "That was your great-grandmother. That was your uncle. They helped build this." That young person may not know all your stories, but they are walking inside your legacy.

There's another side to legacy that we don't talk about enough: emotional and spiritual clean-up. I want you to think about what you DON'T want to leave behind—unspoken debts, unaddressed conflicts, secrets that explode after you're gone, or a trail of broken promises. Part of financial legacy is integrity. It's being as honest as you can about what you owe, what you own, and where you've fallen short. It might even mean apologizing now for some choices you made that impacted others financially, so that people don't discover surprises after you're gone. That's deep work. That's grown folk work. That is also wealth work, because wealth is not only about assets; it's about the health of relationships that carry those assets.

I want to invite you into a powerful visualization. Close your eyes for a moment and picture your own "homegoing celebration"—not in a morbid way, but as a future scene. You're not there physically, but imagine you can watch it like a movie. People are telling stories about you: what you taught them, how you helped them, what they saw you overcome. Then imagine, after the service, a smaller group sitting with a folder labeled with your name. They open it and find your will, your policy information, your WPBS documentation, your asset list, your Legacy Letter. Watch their faces soften with relief. Hear someone say, "They really took care of us. They thought this through." Feel the gratitude in that room. That is part of the future you are building with the choices you make now.

You might be tempted to say, "This is too much. I just want to survive the month." I understand. That's why we didn't start the book here. We started with leaks, stories, maps, one-dollar revolutions, credit, cushions, streams, and family codes. Legacy is not step one; it's a higher step on the same staircase. But here's the secret: thinking about legacy can actually strengthen your day-to-day discipline. When you know you are not just paying bills, you are building memory, it hits different. When you know that every dollar you direct, every document you sign, every WPBS contribution you make has the potential to bless people who haven't even been born yet, your "why" gets stronger. Strong whys build strong habits.

I want to talk directly to that part of you that feels unworthy. Maybe you're thinking, "Who am I to talk about legacy? I don't have much. I made a mess. Nobody will care." That is the voice of shame, and we are not partnering with it. You are not your past overdrafts. You are not your lowest credit score. You are not the worst decision you ever made on a tired night. You are a person awakening to your power, your assignment, and your responsibility. Even if you never own a big house, even if you never become "rich" by the world's standards, you can still leave clarity, blessing, and a piece of a movement behind you. You matter that much.

Let's get practical for a moment. Legacy planning, at a basic level, includes a few key pieces:

- A will or estate plan that clearly states who gets what and who is responsible for what.
- Beneficiary designations on life insurance, retirement accounts, and any accounts that allow them—so money passes directly to people instead of getting stuck in legal traffic.
- Basic life insurance, if at all possible, to cover final expenses and, if you're able, to provide a cushion for your loved ones.
- A simple document (even a handwritten list kept safely) that says where your accounts are, who to contact, and what you wish for your property, digital accounts, and personal items.
- A Legacy Letter that shares your values, your WPBS "why," your hopes for your family, and any guidance you want to leave.

You don't have to finish all of this in one week. But I want you to see the whole picture at once so your mind has something to aim at. Then, just as in other chapters, we break it down. "This month, I will at least list my accounts and beneficiaries." "Next month, I'll schedule a conversation about a simple will." "This year, I will review my life insurance options." It's not about perfection; it's about progress.

Now, imagine the connection between this and your role in WPBS. As the Society grows, there will be structures—co-ops, joint ventures, community funds, ownership shares. Your piece of those will be part of your estate one day. Legacy planning means you decide ahead of time whether your share goes to your children, your grandchildren, a trust for education, or perhaps back into the WPBS community itself to seed opportunities for others. That's advanced-level giving. That's when you go from being just a participant in WPBS to being an ancestor of WPBS.

I want you to breathe deeply and repeat this, even if only in your mind: "My life will not end in chaos. My legacy will not be confusion. I am learning, step by step, to leave things in better shape than I found them." Feel those words settle. That's not hype; that's direction. That's a new line of family code being written across time.

As we move toward the close of this chapter, remember: legacy is built in layers. Your first layer was waking up to where your money was leaking. Another layer was rewriting your inner money stories. Another was crossing from consumer to owner. Another was mapping your money, committing to one-dollar discipline, taming credit, building a cushion of peace, creating new streams of income, and teaching your family while you learn. Legacy planning is a higher layer, but it sits on all the others. It is you saying, "When I'm gone, my progress will not die with me. It will keep talking. It will keep giving. It will keep building."

Carry this affirmation with you: "I am not just living for today; I am building for generations. My paperwork is love. My planning is protection. My participation in WPBS is part of a legacy that will outlive my body and keep my name working in the earth."

Say it when you feel tempted to shove these conversations to "later." Say it when fear whispers that you're not important enough to leave a legacy. Say it when you start that will, when you update that beneficiary, when you make that payment on a policy, when you send your daily dollar into the river of WPBS.

You are not just trying to die peacefully. You are learning how to live with legacy in mind. And when you do that, every day you are alive becomes more meaningful, more focused, and more powerful—for you, for your family, and for a community that is waiting to feel the impact of your yes.

The Journey Continues

If you are reading these words, it means you stayed with me. You followed the leaks. You faced your money stories. You crossed, at least in your heart, from consumer to owner. You began to map your money, move your one-dollar seeds, tame credit, build a cushion of peace, imagine new streams, teach your family differently, and think about legacy in a new light.

I want you to pause and honor that.

You did not just read a book. You let a book read you. You let it ask you questions. You let it tap on old beliefs and gently, sometimes firmly, ask, "Do we still need this?" You let it invite you into a bigger version of yourself.

Nothing changes until something changes.

On the surface, that sounds obvious. But most of us spend years wanting change without actually changing anything. We want more peace with money but keep the same habits. We want better outcomes for our children but speak the same old codes.

We want community wealth but keep our dollars scattered with no assignment.

By engaging this book, you have already started to shift that. Even if your numbers have not yet moved as far as you want them to, your awareness has shifted. Your vocabulary has shifted. Your "default settings" are being rewritten. That invisible work is real.

From this point forward, the key is simple: keep moving.

You do not have to be perfect. You do not have to get everything right. You do not have to turn into a financial superhero by next Tuesday. You simply have to keep taking small, consistent steps in the direction of stewardship, ownership, and community-building. One leak closed. One story rewritten. One dollar reassigned. One conversation handled differently. One document completed.

You will have months where everything goes smoothly and the plan feels easy. You will also have months where life hits you hard and you feel like you are sliding backwards. In both kinds of months, your identity remains the same: you are a builder in training. You are part of something bigger than yourself. You are not alone.

This is not the end of your Money Moves journey. It is the end of the first lap. There will be more books, more tools, more trainings, more WPBS projects, more testimonies. There will also be new challenges, new decisions, new seasons. Through them all, you will have this core truth to return to:

- I am not a helpless victim of money.
- I am a steward of God's resources.
- I am a builder of something that outlives me.

Take that with you. Speak it over yourself. Live into it, imperfectly but sincerely, a little more each day.

The journey continues. And I am honored to have walked this part of the road with you.

How to Use This Book Going Forward

Now that you have read through Money Moves, you might be asking, "What do I do with this now?" That is a good question, and it deserves more than a vague answer.

First, read it again—but differently. The first time through, you were absorbing. The second time through, you are applying. You do not have to reread every chapter in one stretch. Choose one area at a time. You might spend a month living in Chapter One and Chapter Four, tracking your leaks and building your Money Map. Or you might focus on Chapter Seven while you aggressively build your cushion.

Give each chapter "working time" in your life. That means you do not just read and nod; you take at least one concrete action from that chapter. For example, after revisiting the credit chapter, you might pull your credit reports, list your debts, and choose a repayment strategy. After revisiting the family wealth codes chapter, you might change how you answer your child's next money question.

Use the book as a mirror, not a museum. Museums are for looking at things you do not touch. Mirrors are for adjusting what you see. Each time you come back to a chapter, ask, "What is this showing me about my current behavior? What is one next step I can take from here?"

You can also turn key ideas into daily or weekly check-ins. Once a week, you might ask yourself:

Where did my money leak this week?

- Did I give every dollar a job before I spent it?
- Did I move my one-dollar seed?
- Did I take one step toward my emergency cushion, my debt freedom, or my legacy planning?

You do not need a complex system. Even a simple journal or notes app can hold your reflections and decisions. Over time, those brief check-ins will create a written record of your growth. On the days when you feel stuck, you will be able to look back and say, "I may not be where I want to be yet, but I am not where I was."

Finally, let grace and truth walk together. Tell yourself the truth about where you are, without excuses. Then cover yourself with grace as you grow. Shame will try to make you slam the book shut when you slip. Grace will gently say, "Open it again. Begin again." Choose grace.

Using Money Moves with Your Family, Church, or Group

Money is often a silent source of stress in families, churches, and community groups. People shout over politics, theology, and sports, but whisper about debt, overdrafts, and fear. One of the easiest ways to break that silence is to walk through a shared resource together. Money Moves can be that resource.

You do not need to be a financial expert to lead others through this book. You simply need to be willing to model honesty and growth. You can say, "I am learning this too. Let's walk it out together." That posture lowers defenses and builds trust.

If you are using this book in your family, you might pick one chapter per week or per month to focus on. Read it on your own first, then summarize key ideas in simple language at the dinner table. Ask open questions like, "What stood out to you?" "Have you seen this in our family?" "What could we do differently?" Let your children, spouse, or relatives respond without shutting them down. This is not about being right; it is about building understanding.

If you are a pastor or ministry leader, you can turn Money Moves into a class or small group series. Pair each chapter with Scripture, prayer, and time for testimony. Create space for people to share victories and setbacks. Celebrate simple wins loudly. The first saved $100, the first paid-off credit card, the first completed will, the first month of consistent WPBS contributions—these are milestones worth clapping for. They build hope in the room.

If you are a WPBS chapter leader, consider hosting "Money Moves Circles." These can be in living rooms, church fellowship halls, community centers, or online. Each gathering, you revisit one principle and ask two simple questions: "What did you implement since last time?" and "What will you implement next?" Over time, these circles become places of accountability and encouragement.

Remember, when people talk about money, shame often hides in the corners. Your job as a facilitator is to keep the environment safe. Redirect conversations away from comparison and toward personal growth. Remind everyone that this is not about who makes the most, but who is willing to steward what they have.

Used this way, Money Moves becomes more than a book. It becomes a shared language, a shared framework, and a shared turning point for whole communities.

Money Moves Daily Declarations

Your mouth is a steering wheel.

Every day, you are either repeating the old money stories that kept you stuck, or you are speaking new truths that pull you forward. Declarations do not replace actions, but they do reinforce them. They help your mind and nervous system accept a new normal.

You can speak these declarations in the morning, before you check your accounts. You can whisper them before you sit down with your Money Map. You can speak them when you feel tempted to slide back into old patterns. Let them be simple, strong, and sincere.

I am a steward, not a slave.

I am learning to direct my money instead of being driven by it.

Every day, I am closing leaks and opening doors to better decisions.

I am crossing from consumer to owner in my mind, my habits, and my actions.

Every dollar in my life has an assignment that honors God, my future, and my community.

My one-dollar seeds are not small; they are powerful when I move them consistently.

Credit is my tool, not my master. I borrow with wisdom and pay with integrity.

I am building a cushion of peace. I will not live on the edge forever.

My gifts and skills are allowed to create multiple healthy streams of income.

In my family, the old fear and silence around money stop with me. New wisdom and courage begin with me.

I am planning for more than my funeral. I am building a legacy that will bless people long after I am gone.

As I participate in WPBS and other community efforts, I am part of a bigger story of ownership and restoration.

I am not behind. I am beginning again, with understanding.

You do not have to say all of these every day. Choose the ones that hit your spirit the hardest. Rotate them. Write them where you can see them. Let your own spirit hear your own voice speaking life into this area. Over time, you will notice that your internal conversation about money sounds less like panic and more like purpose.

WPBS: Join the One-Dollar Revolution

Throughout this book, you have seen three letters over and over: WPBS. The West Philadelphia Billionaires Society is more than a clever name. It is a long, disciplined yes to a simple question:

What if we, as a people, stopped waiting for rescue and started building our own collective safety nets, assets, and institutions— even if we had to begin with the smallest seed, one dollar at a time?

One person, one dollar a day, is powerful for that one person. It builds identity, habit, and momentum. But one million people, one dollar a day, is a force. It is a river of capital strong enough to carve new paths through stone.

When you choose to participate in WPBS, you are not just "donating." You are deliberately positioning yourself on the ownership side of history. You are joining with others to say, "We will not only spend in our communities; we will own in our communities."

Your consistent dollar-a-day commitment, aligned with the principles in this book, helps create the conditions for:

Personal stability—through better habits, clearer plans, and stronger cushions.

Family transformation—through new wealth codes, better conversations, and actual assets to pass down.

Community elevation—through shared investments in businesses, properties, and institutions that serve and employ our people.

Global connection—through linking arms with others across the African Diaspora who are tired of being consumers in someone else's story and ready to become co-authors in our own.

Participation in WPBS will look slightly different depending on when and where you are reading this. There will be updated processes, local chapters, digital platforms, tools, and structures that grow over time. The details may shift. The core commitment does not.

One dollar a day.

Moved with intention.

Aligned with a shared vision.

If you feel that tug in your spirit as you read this—if something in you says, "I don't want to just read about this; I want to be part of it"—then consider this your personal invitation.

Begin with what you can do today.

Open your Money Map and give WPBS a specific line.

Move your first intentional dollar, even if it feels small.

Then move the next one.

And the next.

As you do, remember: you are not just funding an organization. You are feeding a movement. You are helping to build a future in which our children and grandchildren can walk into banks, clinics, schools, businesses, and community hubs that bear the fingerprints of our collective sacrifice and vision.

This is what it looks like when loose dollars become lasting legacy.

This is what it looks like when we refuse to leave the next generation only with stories of what was done to us—and instead leave them structures built by us.

If you are ready, welcome.

Let's move, together.

About the Author

Aaron M. Montague, MBA, MDiv, MNLP, MTT, MCHt, MSC, is a pastor, life and success coach, certified Christian Finance Coach, Certified Advanced Christian Deliverance Counselor, hypno-trace therapist, veterans' advocate, and founder of Montague Motivational Ministries MX3.

A retired U.S. military Master Training Specialist, Aaron has spent decades teaching, mentoring, and coaching people through trauma, transition, and transformation. He brings together the soul-deep power of Scripture, the science of behavior change, Holy Spirit–led deliverance, and the art of motivational storytelling to help people rewrite their inner scripts and walk into the lives they were created to live.

As a Certified Christian Finance Coach, Aaron equips believers to align their money with their mission—breaking cycles of fear, confusion, and chaos around finances, and replacing them with stewardship, strategy, and Spirit-led wisdom. As a Certified Advanced Christian Deliverance Counselor, he ministers to the root issues behind financial bondage, identity wounds, and generational patterns, helping people experience freedom in both the spiritual and practical dimensions of their lives.

As the visionary behind the West Philadelphia Billionaires Society (WPBS), Aaron champions a bold, simple idea: one million people, one dollar a day, moving together to build community-owned wealth—banks, businesses, clinics, schools, and assets that our children's children can inherit.

He lives out his calling as a husband, father, grandfather, and spiritual father to many, inviting each person he meets to see themselves not as victims of their past, but as builders of a new future.

When he is not writing, teaching, or coaching, you can find him dreaming up new ways to turn pain into purpose, survival into strategy, and loose dollars into lasting legacy—for individuals, families, and the wider African Diaspora.